LITTLE *by* LITTLE

Unlocking a life of Health, Wealth and Happiness.

VUSI **MASHABANE**

Published by RedOystor Books
an imprint of RedOystor Media (Pty) Ltd
  Ground Floor, Lakeview Building,
  1277 Mike Crawford Avenue, Centurion, 0157

www.redoystor.com/Little-By-Little

www.instagram.com/redOystor
www.facebook.com/redOystor
www.twitter.com/redOystor

Book Cover Design: RedOystor Media
Layout & formating: RedOystor Media

Also available on Amazon.com
Available on Kindle and other retail outlets

  ISBN: 978-1-991206-90-9 (Print)
          978-1-991206-91-6 (ePub)
          978-1-991206-96-1 (International)

DEDICATION

To my Guardian Angels

This work I dedicate to our parents, George and Margareth Mashabane, the patriarch and the matriarch of 'The Monarchy', and my family who cheers me up everyday to succeed.

redOystor

London | Johannesburg | New York

Inspired by the story behind the incredible Forest Man of India, Jadav, who single-handedly built a forest, little by little, against the mighty river that was eating up the island and devouring homes. He started planting daily, around 20 bamboo trees. Through unwavering efforts and consistent acts of daily actions, he's built an amazing Forest.

Some said, 'What can one man do against the mighty river?' And in return, he said, 'If you plant every day, you can do a lot....'

This book is crafted as a masterpiece and it's my gift to humanity. We all are striving to be better humans – trying to make our stay under the sun meaningful.

TABLE OF CONTENTS

ACKNOWLEDGEMENTS

"Enjoy the little things, for one day you may look back and realize they were the big things." - **Robert Brault**

Let me firstly start by thanking my awesome wife, Molatelo. Madre, as we affectionately call her, thank you for all the support. My kids Kgosi and Khaya — this success is also theirs. #LongLive _The Monarchy.

My COTH family, led by Apostle MVG and Mother O. You gave me a platform to speak at our National Conference where this book was birthed. I'm forever indebted to you. I cannot forget COTH Polokwane for your immediate love and support. I carry you wherever I go. Leading you is such a joy. Let's do this thing together!

My Office Team, I cannot trade you for anything. To all my friends and business associates where I serve, you are the tonic that enlightens my vision and the reason I wake up every day to serve humanity.

To RedOystor, our editorial team led by Dr Moss Mashamaite and Vukani Nxumalo - your ingenuity is unmatched and your touch has enabled me to deliver a tour-de-force.

With all of you, I share this huge happiness.

Lastly to God, the Sustainer of all things. God, who is my Universal Source and present help and strength at all times.

PREFACE

'Little by little' is a life-long philosophy that has guided me through the ages. Putting one foot in front of the other, one step at a time, and building an 'empire' one brick at a time.

We are told to dream big because big is the only dream worth chasing. But just as we want the grandeur of big dreams, big ideals and big life desires, very often we must also step back to realise that big is really nothing more than little pieces of actions that come together over time.

Little by little is a philosophy that will help you to design, build, and scale your life as though it were an enterprise, leverage your gifts to unlock a life of happiness, health, and prosperity.

Greatness is cumulative! That's where I want to begin this journey with you. A journey that makes success happen not by storm but by episodes. We all strive to be better humans— who are trying to make this world a better place. I do not think that I have accomplished all, but after fifty years of honing principles into my entire being and life, I have reached a place where I can share and impart, which is all I am trying to do in this work.

Every day, we must embrace the stark reality that each one has to do their best to deliver a spell-bounding performance on life's stage. We need to thrive on being the best in the world and be deeply passionate about what we do. That you have to showcase who you are, announcing to the Universe that your mission matters. Your life's assignment is the greatest enterprising venture you have to deliver – even if you haven't recognized that yet. And this under all circumstances.

If you are going to build your Rome, you need to acquaint yourself with the saying that, "Rome was not built in a day."

The end result is going to depend on questions like, 'How invested are you to yourself? How much are you going to be living in the present, living the gift of life granted to you?'

I have seen the careworn eyes of the defeated, and having read biographies, I just thought how close some of them were to victory. I have read Napoleon Hill's *"Think and Grow Rich"*, and always remember his stories and anecdotes.

Usually, when people think they have failed in life or any enterprise, often it is simply because they have not tried again or hard enough. Death is not just an end of life but often an end of effort.

Remember this, that no child was ever born and *bang!* – walked. That would scare everybody out of the maternity ward. We were designed to be static first, then we crawl, and then we walk baby step by baby step, and then we run, and later we fly in a figurative way of speaking.

What I have found out with babies when they learn to walk is that they fall often. But, what I have also found out is that when they fall, they don't cry, they laugh. So if we can be able to learn to laugh between our little by littles, then like little children, we shall be able to enter the kingdom of God or the kingdom of our greatness. Because God is our greatness, reaching to His heights or the heights that He has set for us, having being created in His image after His likeness should be our pursuit, nothing less.

Little by little does not mean that you should run your mission slowly or slothfully. But, of course, hitting the runway as you take off into your future may require one to build an enterprising life that requires some speed. So don't stay too long on the ground; there aren't so many long runways. This might sound like a contradiction, but it shouldn't be because I speak to you about running your life like a business.

Ours is to edge on little by little, until to the end.

Vusi Mashabane

0 IN THE BEGINNING

Finding Fertile Ground

Bietjie bietjie maak meer - **An Afrikaner saying**

As I begin to write this book, it's a day filled with the opulence of summer, an afternoon ablaze with heat. I have just finished reading a fascinating novel written over a hundred years ago. I am an avid reader of books, all types. And this one novel by Alexander Dumas just made my day. I'm not too fond of asthmatic writing, and as I begin to write this book, I am very thoughtful of that. Therefore, I want this book to breathe on its own, but mostly towards you. I am going to share principles, but you know that principles can be rigid and suffocating even though great.

Moshe *Rabbenu's* Ten Commandments were magnificent, but they still have not endeared him to the world after almost 3571 years. Rigidity! 'Thou shall not,' 'thou shall not.' This book is going to be a 'thou shall' book.

Jesus of Nazareth, on the other hand, was a libertarian breathalyser because he mingled stories with principles. That is a little easy on the mind, especially today when the marketplace of ideas is so highly overcrowded. So I want to begin this book by telling you a story, a story about me and where I come from. In other words, I want to inaugurate the narrative at a place of respiration. With the respiratory pandemic that is now plaguing the world, methinks people need to breathe even while they read.

I started very early in my life, not because I was merely brilliant but because I was born amongst teachers, and I was also born with eyes and ears. And other senses of knowledge acquisition too. So I was born a student.

Jesus' command to his disciples was to 'go into all the world and make disciples of all nations. Disciples are students; the word disciple means a learning one. One needs to stay a student, a learning one, to succeed in this life. God has made you multi-sensory; use all of those apparatuses. I've learned from my father, mother, grandmother, brothers, sisters, cousins, and magazines, especially Ebony Magazine, as I will later elaborate.

I have been a scholar of Martin Luther King Junior, self-help books, my Christian faith and teachings, my observation of the world with my eyes and ears and of course other senses, political leaders, civil rights leaders and everything and everybody that pierced into my senses. There is so much to learn in this world; it is simply stupid to be stupid.

We are born with extraordinary gifts and talents, but *tabula rasa*, blank sheets, so those who open themselves to learning have a better chance at success. The most successful people I have ever met had one thing in common—curiosity. They ask questions, and they want to know, and as a result, they peruse books and all sources of knowledge.

The Bible teaches us that the child Jesus grew up in knowledge, in the favour of God and man, and we have never questioned ourselves how he grew up in knowledge. There is only one way; you don't just sit down and eat Kellogg's Cereals and grow up in knowledge. You don't even listen to teachers and acquire knowledge. Teachers give you guidance, but knowledge you must seek and acquire by yourself. What you are taught is guidance; what you acquire or learn by yourself is real knowledge.

"We need to thrive on being the best in the world and be deeply passionate about what we do."

There are no small people in the world. Every one of us has been created in the image and likeness of God, and to refuse to see a man or a woman, because you think he does not matter, can only be done at great expense to yourself.

Little by little – that is the secret of the greats. Steps and not strides. The Bible says that "the steps (not the strides) of a righteous man are ordered by the Lord."

Think about this for a moment, if the Almighty took six days to create the Universe, vast and confounding as it is, why should creating your Universe not take steps. Where I stand, the Almighty could have created the world in one minute or at least one day, vast and confounding as it is, but He didn't.

Perhaps I should now walk you into my story. Before I can even begin to inspire you, you should know who I am and where I come from. I come from the hood. I was born in Soweto fifty years ago to an enterprising father who, under different circumstances, could have become a millionaire. My father was an entrepreneur right down to his boots and a man of infinite resource. My mother was a domestic worker who ensured that white children lived well and grew up to dominate the scene. Imagine growing up to make other people successful and yourself subservient.

I must say this! Nobody must undermine how disabling to the black man, and woman apartheid was. How many possible black giants and success stories were inhibited by it? The migrant labouring that kept my mother and father apart, and in so doing kept us (my siblings and I) apart from our parentage while other races lived together as families is just one thing. The fact that black people could not become anything they wanted to become or trade anywhere they wanted to trade, while other people could do so, is another. Much as we do not want to elevate that circumstance, we must appreciate it. We can't sweep that under the carpet, and we should not be forced and tempted to do so, especially in telling the story of our success or our journey to it.

My father's influence on me as a boy-child, which I will tell you more of, happened mostly during the holiday episodes. Imagine if I had awakened with him every day. But, of course, apartheid was more damaging than we think. But it is our story, and we should never tell our story without it. It is our history as much as the Egyptian slavery and the holocaust are the histories of the Jewish nation, we must not be ashamed to say that some of the South African greatness amongst the blacks was interrupted and inhibited by apartheid, even though greatness is resilient and is able to thrive under all circumstances. Yet many black human forces were sundered by that evil.

If we have succeeded or if we succeed, it is that we have done so, despite it. One mustn't blur the facts when telling the story of where you come from, and I have no intention to bowdlerise my story either. Little by little is that we can, or that you can succeed, in spite of your circumstances.

My father worked as an artisan, but he was always selling various types of fruits and vegetables as a side hustle, depending on the season.

As much as I can remember my childhood, I was always engaged in my father's business when I was in Soweto and my grandmother's fat cakes business when I was in Nelspruit. My father did not just teach me commerce, rands and cents; he often took me on trips to Soweto to show me houses and businesses of successful black people, the likes of Kaizer Motaung, Richard Maponya, Hlongwane and so forth.

When my father took me to successful black people's homes and businesses, he told me that it doesn't matter what the situation is, you can make it under all circumstances. By the way, he did not take me inside their houses because they were not his friends and were mostly highly elevated by their success, and he was a commoner. He was showing me from the outside. He was an outsider to that greatness and wealth, trying to knock on those invisible doors, telling me that I can make it too.

Those men had been able to look unflinchingly at the misfortune of apartheid in the turbulent circumstances of those days and decided to upset it. These were men who pushed their way from obscurity to celebrity.

To me, that was a brigade of believers in God, a breed of the self-believing.

It was fascinating but at that time I was not aware that he was educating me through enterprise tourism, showing me summits of hills he might not have been able to scale himself that he wished for me.

My father was like a Moses saying to me, "I may not reach the Promised Land, but stand on this mountain and see it so that you can strive to reach it." He had that kind of faith in me as all fathers should have in their children. He was teaching me that one should not seek a deputy's seat in this life, that one should seek to be the main man in this world. I clutched my head in sheer bewilderment when I saw the castles and emporiums of those of my black fathers who dared to dream and pursue their goals despite the circumstances.

The entrepreneurial spirit in me was kindled then, never to be quenched. In not so many words, my father taught me that every day, we have to embrace the stark reality that each one has to do their best to deliver a spell-bounding performance on life's stage.

We need to thrive on being the best in the world and be deeply passionate about what we do. That you have to showcase who you are, announcing to the Universe that your mission matters. So your life's assignment is the greatest enterprising venture you have to deliver — even if you haven't recognised that yet. And this under all circumstances.

At that time, I was still a child. I was going to and fro with my father, who had a van during those days. A black man with a car then was a successful person, resourceful and able. So that in itself was a motivating factor for me.

"Remember, Rome was not built in a day."

Let me now take you to a very cliché and important South African saying deliberately prefixed to this chapter. Afrikaners are generally very simple people, but often in their simplicity, there is so much practicality. So much wisdom. Sayings such as '*kos is kos*' (food is food) literally addresses not complaining that your circumstances have reduced you to eating pap and cabbage instead of steak and appreciating that you are not sleeping on an empty stomach. They have had their own hardships too, and at one time, they were in the British concentration camps in this country during the Anglo-Boer War, and I am sure such a saying might have been born there.

However, one of their more famous sayings is, '*bietjie bietjie maak meer*', which translates to "Little by little makes more." Most of us want '*meer*' as '*meer*' is, but '*meer*' is never to be had without '*bietjie bietjie*.'

If you are going to build Rome or a Rome, or your Rome, you must acquaint yourself with the saying that "Rome was not built in a day."

The South African ailment, actually a pandemic, is that we celebrate success instead of progress. We celebrate 'meer' instead of 'bietjie bietjie', the material, the bricks and mortar that create 'meer.'

I will also, in this book, share with you a set of skills that you will need to negotiate a better life for yourself, to live a gainful and fulfilling existence using this same philosophy of little by little. Employing this philosophy, you will still need to be discerning with your time, and if you can build strong values such as; social capital, self-worth, and your passion for your mission, you will go far soon enough.

Because this is a step by step approach to your success and happiness, you will often need to re-imagine the future. As you traverse through life, you will go through things that often cause you to forget about your desired future; however, you need to take some time to reflect, recharge and re-invent. I have had to do that a lot in my life, I have had to take detours, I have had to offload, and I have had to change my script often, but never my direction as in the general pursuit of personal success and fulfilment.

To reach defining moments and destinations that we've set ourselves, we will need to travel light, letting go of things that weigh us down and easily entangle us. It would help if you travelled with less and throw away heaviness and anxiety. Fewer things that are not part of your desired future need to be watched closely and shaken off with the frequency of the necessity of a bath.

There is an epoch of growth, and those who desire to experience newness must never lose heart when they go through troubles, which is a given in this life.

God wants you to go beyond your challenges and begin to see His goodness in the land of the living in spite of those. The capacity to liquidate the past is necessary to success. And that should be done regularly.

If we may, let us get back to my story in the earlier mornings of my life. Having lived in the early 1970s in South Africa, my story is entirely different from that of South Africa's children, even my children today. I will not allow myself an *immunisation* of the emotions when telling it. I like my story, any story, more visceral than cerebral.

I relocated to Nelspruit to live with my grandma because of the chaos of June 16. So born in Soweto, I was raised in Nelspruit, though I always went to Soweto, where my dad was, on holidays.

So the cities I exult to be the native of are Soweto and Nelspruit, a Tale of Two Cities. But if time-spent defines one's home town for me, it would be Nelspruit.

In Soweto, it was never a holiday, we were always engaged in vending my father's wares. Anyway, black people in those days never had the kind of holidays we can have today. Yet the comedic paradox of the day is that we probably had even happier holidays than white people; beaches, safaris and all notwithstanding. In this migrancy, two world views remarkably collided and collapsed into each other—Soweto, where the intellectual life of South Africa was most resolute and eLekazi, which was mostly laid back.

My father was a great reader of newspapers, especially the Rand Daily Mail. So I grew up seeing him read. He was also a hell of a dresser. In him, fashion displayed her charms. The very rustle of his silks was a neighbourhood sigh. I learnt from ogling at him that fine feathers make delicate birds indeed. So I grew up very dressy because of that. I have just toned down now for my new reasons.

Because of my father's reading habits, as soon as I could make do with the English tongue, I began to read books by the moving spirits of the day, the likes of Og Mandino's Greatest Salesman in the World, Norman Vincent Peale, Napoleon Hill and others.

I also took an appetite to the American magazine Ebony, such that at the age of fourteen already, I was ordering it through the Post Office to the amazement of the staff there. During those times, people didn't think you could order anything from overseas and get it. I thought so, and I always got my magazines.

"How invested you are in yourself determines how far you will return true value to yourself."

I was thrilled by the stories of successful black people. When an opportunity came for somebody to go to town and buy things, I was the keenest volunteer because I knew that I would be able to buy a book with the change. Any money I could get, I was interested in nothing else.

I rummaged frenetically through all the success stories of men, especially the black man. So my mind was well-nourished with study very early. My father instilled in me the consciousness that I am Vusi Mashabane, and I am a black person. But, despite all that, I am entitled to maximise my gifts, be enterprising, and ultimately become wealthy and fulfilled. He didn't have to tell me about apartheid. It was all over the show. Even the young eye could see. He just showed me successful black people without showing me white injustice. It was irrelevant to him because success to him was a stronger force.

The apartheid government could not stop him from doing business with his own people. It did not stop Richard Maponya or Kaizer Motaung, or Jomo Sono.

This was a very important perspective. It was the story of Ebony magazine glittering with black success without any negativity. It is not necessary to be negative because social ills will remain with us under any regime. The thing is to concentrate on building your life and living like it was the main business of your world.

My father never emphasised blackness except for its success. He wanted me to know that black people have it within themselves to succeed no matter what. I appreciate that view, and it has stirred me forward in spite of the politics of the day. My old man was simply cultivating my mind with positivity.

The Chinese have proven to us that we can shelve colonial politics and be ourselves and win and eclipse the colonialists even. The African colonial inferiority complex was engendered by the colonialists' need for us to serve them. It was planted at an industrial level, but redemption from that will occur person by person. Every individual would have to redeem himself. We need to reclaim our greatness. We are all great people, and we need to understand that we can achieve that—little by little.

How invested you are in yourself determines how far you will return true value to yourself — be it mental, physical, and spiritual. When you live your life on the path of purpose and mission, you become gainful and fulfilled. The secret is to find the magic that helps manifest it. Then, we can be happy, healthy and wealthy.

Yet again, often life robs us when it diminishes our sparkle.

One of the things that we should not be afraid to applaud is the success stories of blacks in this and any other sphere. Even just black couples who were separated by apartheid's migrant labour system. They might not have been able to achieve success as in wealth, but oh, what resilience! It's always mostly against all odds and that is the beauty of it.

The fact that my father and mother died still married, loving and raising us, is in itself, a powerful success story. In a way, I am still a migrant, I travel a lot because of business, but at least this is not a forced one. But I have learned from my upbringing that it should not affect my wife, my children, and my family's overall well-being.

If I am anchored as a family man, it is because of my father and my mother. Without drifting to the political, the structure of the black household was the most attacked by the white establishment, and we survived it because we concentrated on the basics. This book is going to be, in the main, about the basics that will help you to be able to scale the heights you dream of.

1 SEED PLANTING

Investing in Your Life

It's a small price to pay, but investing a little extra effort into the life you choose will move you from average, where all the competition is, to the top - **Richie Norton**

To master yourself, you must first know yourself. I believe that the greatest failure of the modern school system is based on the fact that they teach everything else but the knowledge of self.

It was Ralph Waldo Emerson who brought this to a sharp focus that *'To be yourself in a world that is constantly trying to make you something else is the greatest accomplishment.'* Self-knowledge should have preceded locusts and lizards in all the education systems. Then, our human capital and advancement would have been at its zenith.

At the doors of the mystery temples of ancient Egypt, where

Moses of the Pentateuch and the Torah received his learning, was written in bold script, 'Know thyself.'

This is the greatest maxim for a higher life. That statement alone is supposed to be at the prefix of the beginning of an education. This was the birthplace of the first civilization whose pyramids can still not be eclipsed by mathematical exactness today, thousands and thousands of years later.

The Greek philosophers who mostly studied their philosophy in the same Egyptian mystery temples, then appropriated the statement, as in plagiarised it; today, when you say or quote that statement, it is given to the Grecians, when it was actually a Kemetic or ancient black Egyptian maxim.

"'Know thyself', speaks to personal knowledge and self mastery."

Know thyself' speaks to personal knowledge and mastery. Personal mastery is paramount to one's ultimate journey towards happiness, health and the building of wealth, and at the highest echelon, the changing of the world, which should never leave exactly the way we found it if we are descendants of Deity, whatever the name we ascribe to it.

I remember when I went to school, they taught us about locusts, lizards and ants. I still don't know why. Of all things in the world, why locusts, lizards and ants? They did not even tell us, at least that locusts were very high in protein. Or that ants were very enterprising by nature. That could have helped somebody. But, I never have in my life found myself in a corner where I had to answer those questions (the anatomies of locusts, lizards and ants) to save my life or to put food on my table.

I believe that the drop-outs of the school system are victims of that; they overlook that self-knowledge is perhaps more important than locusts, lizards and ants.

Nobody should drop out of the school system if the system pursued self-knowledge first and foremost. No child has come to the world to offer nothing; nobody is born to be excluded from success, health or wealth or happiness, or some form of greatness, for that matter.

If the school system first evaluated the gifts and talents of every child before they began educating, the world would be a different and marvellous place for everyone. Remember that the instruments of the school system perceived guys like Thomas Edison and Dr Ben Carson as way below average children.

The conveyor belt of that system evaluates people with the same criteria, and the people who fall off the belt are regarded as below average or failures. That conveyor belt has thrown off many a genius throughout time.

If they get to believe the verdict of that system, then they are relegated to a life of failure no matter what their potential and genius were. Albert Einstein said, "Education is what remains after one has forgotten what one has learned in school."

At 15 already, Einstein clashed with the authorities and

resented the school's regimen and teaching method. As a result, a good number of students dropped out of school at the time, and they were labelled failures.

Why would anybody be born and be a failure at such a tender age? To be born is an act of triumph. I do not need to share the cliché story that you had to beat and be ahead of billions of sperm cells to be born. That is cliché already.

The greatest neurosurgeon who ever lived, Dr Ben Carson, a genius, was regarded as stupid by her teachers until her mother discovered that he had a sight impediment and because he could not see well, he could not cope with the lessons.

"It is the genius of God that he has been able to create billions and billions of beings and none the same.

Likewise, the story of Thomas Edison, the great inventor, is well known to the world. The guy whose mother was told by a teacher through a letter that he was a waste of time and incapable of learning proved to be one of the greatest inventors who ever lived.

The school system could not identify that, and that genius could have easily fallen off the conveyor belt were it not for a mother who believed in her child.

Mass production is wrong at the human level because no two human beings will ever be the same. You cannot mass produce humans. It is in the human form that we are unique.

It is the genius of God that he has been able to create billions and billions of beings and none the same.

The school system is trying and has been trying to mass-produce things that cannot be mass-produced. I suggest that the departments of education all over the world must go into the baked beans business, produce them, can them and retail them and get out of the human business.

I am of the view that education or the education system in its current form is not adequate to prepare one for the journey of life. This is why I strongly believe in self-education as the best kind of education you can administer to yourself. And *self* education cannot be mass-produced. It is tailored to your need, desires and aspirations. Every part of *self* education feeds into the little pieces of your life's puzzle and is at the heart of personal growth and development.

Our indomitable spirit, which is our fuel, thrives when we face our challenges with greater courage, even in the face of great adversity. In one of his poetic writings, William Ernest Henley suggests in 'holding on to one's own dignity despite the indignities life places before us to demonstrate the outlook we need to embrace to grow and to survive.' Rising above what is currently offered in terms of knowledge and education so we can become disciples of our destiny. Only then can we become masters to ourselves.

The way to develop a sense of personal mastery is to approach life as a discipline, and this is what Peter Senge brings out in his work, "The Fifth Discipline."

Discipline, to me, means that you are constantly aware of what you are doing, and you are constantly directing what you are doing and aware of and managing the outcomes. Peter Senge says in his tour de force, "what we see manifesting outwardly in us is largely orchestrated intrinsically in what we place at the centre of our heart or spirit and soul."

According to the Holy Book, the wisest who ever lived on earth, King Solomon, admonished us centuries ago that we should 'guard your heart with all diligence for out of it are the issues of life.'

Likewise, the New International version of the scriptures says to "guard your heart, for it is the well-spring of life."

The heart in the Bible is interchangeable with the spirit and the soul together. So when the Bible says 'heart', it is speaking about what Peter Senge calls 'head and heart, spirit, soul and mind.'

"Again 'Know thyself' is very paramount to living a life of infinite possibilities."

"People with high levels of self-mastery cannot afford to choose reason and intuition, or head and heart, any more than they would choose to walk on one leg or see with one eye."

In other words, he is appealing to a multi-sensory approach that completes the human experience and is necessary for us to achieve our ultimate goals.

We are not our bodies, even though our bodies are essential for our sojourn in this world. We are a composite of spirit, body and soul, and unfortunately, we have mostly neglected some aspects of our beings, which is not very helpful to successful living.

Another thing that was not to be missed from those great teachers was alignment to a Higher Power. Dr Peale and Og Mandino call this Higher Power, God. Napoleon Hill calls it the Subconscious Mind. I say to you today, that a rose by any name still smells sweet. A concept of a higher power exists in all cultures.

Everything else is semantics. So, universally we might disagree about all things, but this probably, the Higher Power, is what connects us all.

Be that as it may, when our souls are aligned to a Higher Power, our purposes can produce tremendous results that would make our lives worth living and truly enjoyable.

Life is meant to be enjoyable. So why would the universe take you out of nothingness and usher you into a world of misery? How sadistic could God be, or if you please the gods? My take is that we are the ones who make our minds and our lives.

The secret is with us, as in the ball is in our court. Being created in the image of God, we are the creators of our own worlds, so if we come out short, it is simply our own shortcomings.

Investing in your life guarantees growth in the areas you invest in, and growth is not only a proof of life but an imperative. It is a principle of life that what does not grow ultimately dies. Growth is a beautiful thing.

Have you ever observed children grow, trees and flowers grow, businesses grow, and economies grow?

I have spent time just observing a flower blooming from a bud, and I thought it was the most beautiful thing I have ever observed. It was videotaped by, I believe, National Geographic.

Wealthy people do not invest because they are rich. On the contrary, they are rich because they invest or get rich because they invest. In like manner, a life worth living, a life you can personally be proud of, a fulfilling life, is born out of the investment you make into it.

The question should now be, what are these things that I should invest in my life? Obviously, these things must be items of value. So as you go through this volume, you will pick up gems of investments that I will keep throwing at you as I unravel this narrative.

The first investment has got to be time. To live is not to breathe away your time. I have heard people talking about whiling away time. Perhaps let me suggest that time is probably the last thing in your life you would want to while out.

To live is to watch and guard what your time does for you, jealously. Time is the only equalizer in life. Successful people and unsuccessful people alike have been allocated twenty-four hours a day. The difference is what the two types do with it. Little by little also means daily or one day at a time.

This book brings to bear how to calibrate your soul to your source of success, a Higher Power, in that way creating a life of wonder. This aligns you with your purpose, and you thrive even more when you are in sync with your environment and totally aligned with the divine.

In the pages that follow, I share how ancient wisdom has assisted great powers and nations accentuate their existence into meaning and significance. It provides profound yet straightforward universal views that life is our most treasured asset; therefore, we must invest in it. No one has a crystal ball, and life doesn't always promise that it will be profitable in all its ventures.

So there are no guarantees on how eventually things will pan themselves out. The beauty about little by little is that everybody can do it. You see, I am not preaching that you should become a genius or start rich or great. I am saying invest and begin with the little that you've got.

The guarantees I bring with me in this book are that mountains are made out of pebbles, not out of other mountains. The atom, no matter how small, is still the element of greatness.

There is an American popular story of a pastor who bought a piece of land. Worked it, tilled it, until it was a thing of beauty and very productive. When a member of his congregation saw it, he exclaimed with great wonderment and said, 'Reverend isn't it wonderful what he the good Lord can do!' The Reverend looked at him and shook his head with annoyance, and said, 'Son, you should have seen it when the good Lord still had it all by Himself.'

A few years ago, a famous Japanese philosophy was popularized by American management gurus called 'Kaizen', and it meant in the common tongue, 'improve yourself daily.' 'Japanese products and technologies used to be some of the poorest in the world.

The term *maJapan* was today's equivalent of *Fong Kong*. But they broadly applied this philosophy until their products and technologies today are amongst the best in the world. There is nothing that can't be improved upon except God. So when I first heard of the concept of cleaning water, and I am talking about seemingly clean crystal water, I was non-nonplussed. Could water be improved upon?

I am an African and was raised with stories around the evening fire. While often told in anecdotes and allegories, the wisdom of my ancestors was often simplified in folklore; that way, every child could learn. That reached me too because I want to believe that I am every child, and for me, that is the height of communication.

Personal mastery is key to one's ultimate journey towards happiness, health and the building of wealth."

As I connect with you in this book, I will use scenarios and stories to elaborate on some life issues. I am every child who happened to learn a couple of things along the way on my path and I think that every child, if they incline their ear to hear, can become something out of what I am going to share in this treatise.

I am sure that there are many reasons why Jesus used parables that related to the communities he preached to. Buddha was also known for using parables to communicate his wisdom, so was Confucius and Mohammed.

Teaching is, to me, an art as well as a science. Where I come from, I am neither an artist nor a scientist; I am just a teacher and storyteller who hopes to benefit you from my life experiences. I am a good learner too, and I have read notes from many gurus, griots and teachers, and I have greatly benefited from that. But to me, Christ was the greatest teacher of all times.

I have learnt very much from Christ's lessons and style, and for that, I do not want to lose those lessons and that wisdom. So allow me to follow his example.

Allow me to tell a few stories in this book to soften the complex principles, the Laws of Moses, of Confucius, of Siddhartha Gautama, if I might so call them. Allow me to reach out to you at the level of ordinariness. I am talking ordinariness because I have not attained the status of the people I have just mentioned. I am simply a disciple, and because of that, I am at your level. And I think because of that you can understand me as in, I can communicate successfully with you.

A little bit about me and my life story, many years ago, as a young school kid in Thembeka High School, Ka Nyamazane, I began to grow an appetite for self-help books and material, and I decided to join and be part of a church too.

My appetite for self-help books led me to read Og Mandino's "The Greatest Salesman In The World" and his other books, Peter Senge and Dr Norman Vincent Peale. In addition, Napoleon Hill's

"Think and Grow Rich." Kenneth Hagin's numerous publications fascinated me with plenty to learn.

I gained much knowledge of the world around me from Oral Roberts's healing and evangelistic publications, George S Clason's classic, "The Richest Man in Babylon", and the biography, material and speeches of Dr Martin Luther King Jr., and of course, the Holy Bible and much more. Obviously, we are here talking about a *'cyclopaedia'* of information to bombard a young and keen soul, which is me more than thirty-five years ago.

If knowledge is power, I was greatly empowered that early.

These great authors and motivators fascinated me, the reader and held me rapt. I was therefore raised with principles, tales and anecdotes from that copious store.

Since there was a dearth of books and there were no real libraries in our black society, I read most of those books over and over again.

I must say that it was a blessing in disguise because reiterating that kind of material in my head could only be good for me. And it is reading the right materials repeatedly that leaves a lasting impact on one's life.

I also read my school books too but to be honest with you, there was not much I could extract from them to help me in real life. Most school books and real life are not related at all.

A friend of mine once told me that the person who started what we call education in this world was an evil genius. There is no easier way to control the world except with that which we call education. Unless in societies that love their children and their futures more than they love themselves, an education system can be a very, very dangerous thing.

Education must be crafted by a father and a mother who love and believe in their children because only nature must nurture its children. To trust political parties with your children's education is to be truly naïve. They want to win the next election, and all their doings are towards that.

As much as you are responsible for the physical nurturing of your children, shouldn't you take responsibility for what goes into their heads? Are your children's stomachs more important than their heads? Why do you want somebody else to be entirely responsible for the better part of their being while you call yourself a parent? Abdicating our responsibilities is the bane of parenthood.

Investing in your life is also investing in your children because they are your life. No parent is ever going to be successful when your children are failures.

To succeed as a parent can only be viewed holistically. That is why ideally, people have to be matured adults to begin to think of parenting.

In the days of the Apostle Paul and previous, when you were an intelligent person, you would be apprenticed to a proven wise man like Paul learnt at the feet of one Rabbini Gamaliel, so did most of the Renaissance greats, artists, poets, authors. They were apprentices of proven greatness. Plato was an apprentice of Socrates, a proven philosopher, and he was also an initiate of the Egyptian mystery temples.

Education then was not used to meet political ends. But,

unfortunately, the current school system forces you to learn from people who have nothing to brag about in learning and greatness. I once observed a very disturbing scene. This gentleman was trying to sell books to a teacher at a school, and the teacher said, 'Me, I don't read.' Imagine being apprenticed to people who have nothing to offer to you. Teachers who only read the books they are going to teach from.

I have been a university student and sat under men and women that I could teach, even as I freshly graduated from High School. And these people had to decide whether I passed or not. That was the system.

If I think the way I do, it has nothing to do with that system, I am simply being original and critical. And as I have already mentioned, I also learnt from proven greatness with a little more particularity.

"Discover your dream life and live happily ever after, albeit with flaws."

That we have to pay so much money for such futile exercises is tragic, to say the least. I am done with critical thinking and observations (laugh).

Dr Martin Luther King was particularly the single most significant influence in my literal work. In a manner of speaking, I sat down under his feet even though he died before I was born. I devoured everything that was written about him and that he wrote and spoke, greedily. I named my firstborn son *Kgoši* after him, which is King in the Sepedi language, my son's mother tongue.

Do not forget Og Mandino, Dr Norman Vincent Peale, Napoleon Hill and others. What kept popping out from these different materials, from these great teachers and thought-leaders, was that 'to get somewhere in life, to climb to the heights of your hairiest and most audacious dreams and goals, you've got first to *master yourself.*' So they made it very clear to me that my success depended on none other than myself.

When you get to that place in your life, there is no need for excuses; there is no need to blame circumstances and others. Whether you are born an orphan or born black in a country that diminishes blackness is no longer important. What is important is that you are you, son of God, Creator of the universe.

If this was a movie, I mean your life a movie, it would be a very intriguing story of a movie because you start from the bottom, and your life-story is therefore bound to be epic.

There are many people who came from humble places who made it to the presidency of the United States of America. However, none was as illustrious as that of President Barack Obama. Why? Because all the odds were against him. The white house was never meant to be a '*black house*', and it had no such dreams.

As I traverse this thought, Sylvester Stallone comes to mind. He created and acted in Rambo and Rocky. What made those movies unforgettable was that the odds were so stacked against the main character that it was not funny. Yet, in those epic tales, he demonstrated the power of the human spirit against all odds.

When you follow his real-life story, you know that he derived the wisdom that shaped those great episodes from his own real life. Of course, he made other beautiful movies, but none would ever surpass the two for their *heroicness.*

The Apostle John says, "I write to you young men because you are strong, and the word lives in you and you have overcome the evil one." To be strong doesn't mean that you are not afraid. If anything, when your dream doesn't scare you enough, perhaps it's not that big.

Being strong doesn't mean you will not trip. Yet what it means is that you can pick yourself up and move on. Being strong means pushing your fear out of your way and let faith lead you. So, today you can discover your dream life and live happily ever after, albeit with flaws.

I must go back to my self-help reads, the Og Mandino's et al. You had to read those books with your head in your skull. The messages were not necessarily overt, and you had to read and read and often read between the lines. One of the most difficult ones was Napoleon Hill's "Think and Grow Rich." He just kept suspending you, teasing you and not getting to the point. But when he did get to the point, did he just get to the point? Yes, he did!

So you could say that I began to invest in my life from a very early age. At that time, I did not necessarily know that I was making an investment. So I can say that I was just curious and hungry, the curiosity and hunger aroused in me by my father, who was an avid reader of newspapers.

The saying, 'knowledge is power,' is simply an understatement, especially when talking about the right type of knowledge. It is the power of that knowledge that is propelling my life even today. A graduate is a product, and often we pride ourselves in being products of factories that are no good.

The fact that education is decided upon by politicians and politics makes it a very dubious institution in our world. It is therefore essential to augment it with self-education.

I advocate self-education, and I do not take any man or woman seriously whose last read book was the one prescribed while studying for a Diploma or a Degree. I am not saying that education is terrible. It teaches us literacy and numeracy. Once in a while, you find an illuminated teacher who will use that moment to inspire you. However, I am for self-education because you are you and nobody else. Bantu education, which was introduced in South Africa in 1953 proves that what we so quickly call education can have a sinister agenda.

An agenda not to uplift but to undermine what we are. What makes us think the current education that is being dished out to our children is well-meaning. This brings me to the fact that self-education might be the best kind of education you can administer to yourself. My children go to excellent schools, but I still make it a point that they learn more out of school than in, just like myself.

I want to suggest that the school curriculum, any school is not sufficient for you. I am not saying that it is a waste of time; I am just saying it is inadequate. It is like the food that we eat now. It is so insufficient that one has to augment it with supplements to stay healthy.

Of course, there are those who believe that we are descendants of apes. They are within their rights to think that. However, I do have a problem with that kind of thinking. It makes it tough to motivate yourself to greater aspirations if you reduce your origins to apes. I want to look up to the place where I come from, I would like to look up to a Higher Power, and I have seen greatness come from that kind of outlook.

The plagiarizing Greeks who are honoured by those who don't know as the initiators of the first-ever civilization were *Khemetian* initiates. They learnt everything they ever knew from black Africa. Worse even, some of the great quotations attributed to them were coined in Africa by great African minds.

Western historians refuse to give praise to Africa because if they did so, Africa could rise. And this is not just political speak, these are facts. It is with that reasoning that I devalue education because it has always come with an agenda. Let's go back to Egypt again, and I will give you a little appraisal of that ancient land. Jesus comes out from Egypt at the age of twelve, and he confounds the priests with his knowledge and wisdom.

At the age of eighty, Moses comes out of Egypt, and he gives his people the Five Books of the Law. Whenever an economic depression or famine hit Abraham, Isaac and Jacob, they went down to Egypt.

They had some robust education down there, and the Jewish and other peoples of the world benefited greatly. Where I come from, you can inherit thrones and wealth, but not success. True success can only be born out of a personal pursuit, and one's fulfilment should never be outsourced to life's intermediaries. As much as nobody is born a failure, nobody is born a success; success must be achieved, just as failure is achieved.

Painfully, growing up in Soweto, I saw, at an industrial level, people born in the same place under the same conditions, producing variegated and far-flung results. It was a lesson that, as a child, I found puzzling. You had Kaiser Motaung, Richard Maponya and Mr Hlongwane in a sea of mediocrity and poverty, and I asked myself what is wrong with this picture?

But my teachers (from the literature I read) kept showing me that things like environment and circumstances are plastic, that the main factor in my world is me, and that mastering this factor is my key to my desired future. The problem and the solution to my desired future was the same. The same guy I see when I look into the mirror.

By so saying, I mean that the key is within you, not out there. The failures and successes of the *Sowetans* were all within themselves. The Kaizer Motaungs, the Jomo Sonos and the Richard Maponyas of this world are not fortunate as fortune flies in the skies. They are fortunate because they created their fortunes by themselves.

I heard a story from somebody who used to work for Eskom a few years back. He told me that they ordered electrical globes from Japan with the special order they would only allow and accept 5% defective products in the range.

Apparently, the Japanese manufactured and processed their order as requested, and when it arrived, there was a smaller container on the side.

The products in the bigger containers were all perfect. When they called back to their suppliers and asked what the other container was for. They were told that in their order, they had asked for 5% defective globes.

They said we thought that is what you wanted; we manufactured them according to your specs.

The Japanese were not trying to be funny. They might have been amused, but they did not understand why Eskom, South Africa, would want 5% faulty globes because they don't manufacture defective globes, as a matter of principle.

But you see, the Japanese did not start there, at this place when they are not even able to comprehend humans' lowering of standards. Instead, they started little by little, as in *Kaizen*, believing in improvement instead of improvising. So there is a significant difference between the two words, even though I don't mean to insinuate that the word 'improvising' is a bad word at all.

"True success can only be born out of a personal pursuit of life long dreams."

Today what began in Japan revolutionized the entire oriental block. Now South and North Korean products, Chinese products, are amongst the most demanded in the world. China has specifically become the manufacturing capital of the world for everything.

They can give expensive quality products and cheap inferior products according to your needs. It is in China where the customer is always right. If you want poor and cheap, they give you poor and cheap. If you want the best quality, they give you just that.

Raymond Schwab wrote a book, "The Oriental Renaissance," and he said that it was the discovery of India and other eastern countries by Europe, or rather the discovery of their ancient civilizations by Europe, that triggered the renaissance. This whole discovery thing of others by the west is annoyingly untrue.

There was no discovery to talk about and no renaissance in that. For me, the oriental renaissance was when Japan began to apply *Kaizen*, 'improve yourself daily.'

The little by little applications by the easterners have changed the world as we know it. It has changed the world, it has changed the way the world looks at them, and it has also changed the lives of many individuals.

Another thing was when they refused to be pushed out of the things they had learnt in their past. Their history and their heritage. Unlike in Africa, where almost all culture and heritage were forced out of us, and we allowed it. Because of those bold steps, poverty has been pushed to the borders of non-existence in those spheres by a philosophy that says, to eat an elephant, you can only do it one bite at a time. But bite you must, for if you don't bite, the elephant will remain eternally in your sight.

Coming closer home, there is a Sepedi saying that goes, '*Kodumela moepa thutse, ga go lehumo le le tswago kgauswi*,' which literally translated means, Keep digging, wealth digger, there is no wealth to be dug out from the near surface, or sweat it out gold digger, nobody has ever lazed his way to riches.

Even the sophisticated prefabs of China are made step by step, so is a life worth living. "The Journey of a thousand miles begins with one step," said the wise Lao Tzu.

Let the reading of this book be the start of that journey, the journey of a thousand miles if you have not yet embarked on it or are halting at the starting point. If you were already on this journey of living your life as an enterprise, be encouraged and let us continue because this is the only way to go upwards. Little by little is a philosophy of life that I want to introduce to you until we build it into a movement. I want to convert you into being a disciple of small beginnings.

It is perhaps one of the simplest philosophies of life to health, wealth and happiness. I say that because little children apply it intrinsically to learn everything they do, including mere walking, talking, and everything else. So if little children can do little by little, we all can.

Keep living the present, the gift you were bestowed by God, who trusted you to make the most of it. When people do wonderful things, they are said to be gifted.

I say, to live or to be born is to be granted the greatest gift of all –life. But, there is one thing that I want to tell you, and that is, the fact that you picked up this book means that you are a winner. You won the first day you were born, but you won again the day you picked this book up and ogled into the words written in it.

I am not saying that everybody will become a Martin Luther King, my idol, or a Moses of the Pentateuch. All I am saying is that everybody can attain health, wealth and happiness and a level of greatness and positive influence in the world that I believe is our heritage as humans if indeed we were created in the image of our God.

Robert F Kennedy said on the Day of Affirmation address

delivered at the University of Cape Town, South Africa, June 6, 1966, "Few will have the greatness to bend history itself, but each of us can work to change a small portion of events, and in the total of all those acts will be written the history of this generation," and I concur.

When Jesus Christ taught the masses of Galilee of the Chaldees to pray, he said to them, "When you pray, do so in this wise, "Our Father who art in heaven, ..." If the One who created the universe is your father, what heights can you reach in this world or perhaps a rephrase, what heights can you not reach in this world?

Little by little, I am saying to you that anybody can scale the heights applying this philosophy.

Little by little is not only cute. The beauty of littleness is that it is achievable by anyone. This is why I preach that philosophy because it is not above any living and breathing person. Allow me to throw in a paradox at this stage. Littleness is greatness, but only when done repeatedly.

Today's philosophies are reached only by the brilliant, the high and the mighty, the privileged of this world. I assure you that this is not one of them. The oak, the mother and giant of all trees, was once only an acorn.

Jesus talks about, "If you have faith as a mustard seed you shall say to this mountain, be thou removed and be thou cast into the sea...." May I tell you the size of a mustard seed and the mountain he was speaking about? This mountain he was pointing at?

The great evangelist and healer Oral Roberts I hear got inspiration from God to build a university. He called in a few of his supporters and followers in Tulsa, Oklahoma, to a meeting. After preaching, he announced that he would build a university and asked for an offering from the congregation.

The money raised was only about twenty-six dollars. He prayed over the offering and said that he was going to build a university with that money. With the twenty-six dollars that he received, he did not only build a university; he built The City of Faith, the Prayer Tower and other massive structures.

They say that before Oral Roberts came to the place today called South Tulsa, it was a bush.

This is the story of the mustard seed, the story of small things. We were all not born grown; we grew. What makes us think that anything, anything at all, could just suddenly be grown? Even writing this book could only be done little by little, line by line until there is a page; page by page until there is a chapter; chapter by chapter until there is a book. There is no other way of going around it.

"Though you started with little, so prosperous will your future be." - Job 8:7

When I grew up in the Lowveld and Soweto as a Christian, there was one word that I hated most – patience. I loved instant coffee, instant anything; the process was one thing that I did not like. I did not want to wait for anything. And I thought the success of people like Richard Maponya and Kaizer Motaung crept upon them instantly. According to my little eyes, when they opened, these men were successful, and I thought that they were always successful. I thought that they woke up one morning, and there they were.

What a poor view of the machinations of the world that we live in! Even Christ Jesus himself, the Bible says, "He grew in favour with God and man."

Growth is a process, never instant. It does not matter where you are or who you are today. I guarantee you one thing, that you can grow. You can grow or (better) your health, your wealth and your happiness. And the approach is the cliché, 'how do you eat an elephant?' One bite at a time.

I know that elephants might not like that, but I think I have made my point.

Children can teach us something in this respect. Have you ever heard the little ones talk about when they grow up? They say when I grow up, "*I want to become....*" They know that when you truly grow up, you become, and they look forward with great anticipation to that, to growing up.

Little by little is more about becoming, not necessarily being. The pleasure is in the journey∎

2 EMPIRE BUILDERS

Living A Legacy

The empires of the future are the empires of the mind. - **Winston Churchill**

The word 'build' is a great word. It carries enormous weight whenever it has been used.

I have always *marvelled* at buildings and city-scapes. I've admired builders too. I have often stood long and watched men and women working at large construction sites. Although at one time it looks messy and disorderly, you would not be able to imagine that a thing of beauty will emerge out of the seeming chaos.

That is how much I am in love with those structural beauties.

The mathematics, the engineering, the science and the diligence all intrigue me. Buildings are an admixture of art and science, just like music. The time factor to buildings is also very crucial. You don't mix mortar and go out for lunch.

You've got to be on the ground; you've got to be time-based. You can't be laid back and try to build at the same time.

The word empire is an even greater word than building. Countless books have been written about the epic imagery of these two words – building and empire.

The word you, the name of you, dear reader, is at the pyramid of greatness compared to the other words I have just mentioned. Let me start with the word build. It is a great word. We are here to build. We are here to build structures that will be here long after we are gone.

In the African culture, there is a game that children play called *Mandlwatane*. In English, they call it *'playing house.'* Like most children, I played this game while growing up. In this game, the boys build houses, girls cook food, and they enjoy themselves. The goal is to build the best house, bring or cook the best food. Little children do this. It is a joyous experience as children begin to grow the concept of building, family, success, and progress.

Children are builders, and we should take our cue from them. These children have the mind and capacity of builders. There is an element of future and training. Let's appreciate that. What I find fascinating about this is how they get so absorbed by what they do. Christ said, if you be not like little children, you shall not see the kingdom of God.

May I suggest that this is the age of the empire builders? No, no, may I rather insist that this is the age of the empire builders? May I usher you personally into the era of empire builders? By so saying, I mean to co-opt you because there is no reason why you should not be one of them, as in one of us?

And when I say one of us, I hope you do not misconstrue me to mean that I say that I have already built an empire. On the contrary, like the Apostle Paul, I say unto you that I have not yet attained, I am still pressing on, yet I am an empire builder. I am building, and I have a lot that I can show for it.

An empire is a large scale of real estate, presence and influence. To say I am building is better testimony than that I have built it because empires are not small structures, whether spiritual or material. What I know is that I am building mine, present continuous tense, and I am inviting you to yours. So rather than try to teach you in this chapter, I am simply and only inviting you to join me, to join us.

Let us walk together in this journey of the building of our empires. Empire builders do not go into life or business with the narrow mind of just eking out a living. Instead, they go out with swelling ideas, unafraid of circumstance and this life as it was handed over to us.

Alvin Toffler, the author of the tour de force "Future Shock" said, "it is better to err on the side of daring than the side of caution."

Empire builders are not cautionary in approach but daring. Therefore, join this fearless crew fearlessly, for as the Good Book readily proclaims, "God has not given us the spirit of fear but of love, of power and of a sound mind."

I saw an anonymous quote that I got endeared to another day, and it read, 'Start with nothing, build an empire, leave a legacy.' I thought about that old little song that was sung when I grew up, 'Three little words. I Love You' by David Loggins. (In this regard, phrases) "Start with nothing, build an empire, leave a legacy."

I love the three little phrases a lot.

What are empires anyway, if we may ask? Are they spaces where man dominates another or the others? Are they slave sweat-shops or where the rich and elite dominate and subdue more impoverished people or states?

When I mention the word empire, who comes to mind. What people would you think about? Shaka Zulu? Napoleon Bonaparte? The Holy Roman Empire? A Roman Emperor or a Caesar?

God forbid? The word empire's origin is the Latin *'imperium'*, which means to command, control, dominion, sovereignty.

"It is better to err on the side of daring than the side of caution."

I believe that was one of God's first commandments to mankind without the *middle manning* of a Moses, God talking to Adam *mano a mano*.

In my context, by empire, I am talking of a kingdom or domain, microcosm to macrocosm. The two m's mean that at both levels, micro to macro, you can create your own empire in whatever domain you want to operate in or express your gifts.

I am saying to you, that the word empire should belong in your dictum and dictionary. It should not by any means be foreign to you. It is a big word in any dictionary but so are you.

You can create an empire in any field. In sports, in religion, in the retail business, in the arts, in recreation, in fashion, in literature, in film, in entrepreneurship, in consulting, in childcare, in cuisine, in education; hell, in every field of human endeavour you prefer.

When I talk about empire builders, I am thinking in a no-limits space. I say that you also can command authority, control and dominion in a field of your chosen passion. It is built in human genetics to be able to do so—any human.

Empires are like galaxies, infinite and perhaps even unfathomable except by those who dare! There are empires built hundreds of years ago that still exist today in the banking industry, insurance industries, politics, *restauranting*, health, cosmetics, hair care, hygiene, and any other field you may think of. They have been passed on from generation to generation, and because knowledge was also transferred *trans-generationally*, the empires never perished but instead grew and adapted to the changing of times.

And like it is said by scientists, that galaxies are still being created by the words of God that reverberated in the beginning of time, empires are creatures that are designed or can be created without end.

When I talk about empires, I am talking about a mentality where you say to yourself, I am getting into this space, and I do not want to be a fringe player. Empire thinking is when you say, I want to play in this industry, but I do not want to be a fringe player. I do not want to be on the bench and play when the leading players are injured.

Even better, the greater thinking is the thought that you can create an entire industry on your own — A whole new industry, a new form that never existed before.

Man created the industrial revolution. So is the so-called fourth industrial revolution. The internet industry was kick-started by an African mathematician and computer scientist, the Nigerian Phillip Emeagwali.

Empire creation is more than anything a mentality. It was Napoleon Bonaparte who said, "In this life, we are either Kings or pawns, Emperors or Kings." In the game of chess, there are more pawns than other pieces, so it is in the world of man.

A pawn is a chess piece of the smallest size and value with the most limited movement. Just make up your mind that you are not going to be one amongst them. But even a pawn can be promoted to any other piece if it reaches the opponent's end on the board.

If we are indeed the sons of God, the King of all the galaxies, it means that we could, in our own right, build kingdoms and empires of our own. There is a scripture in the Holy Book that says that the world is yearning for the manifestation of the sons of God. These are empire builders, 'the sons of God.' God is a creator, the Creator, and in a simplistic way of putting it, a builder. His sons can only take after him. It is in the divine gene, and according to all Holy Books, we have been created in His image and after His likeness.

King David in *Psalm 8:3-5 (Common English Bible)* says to God in praise and great psaltery, "When I look up at your skies, at what your fingers made— the moon and the stars that you set firmly in place—What is man that you keep him in mind? The son of man that you take him into account? You've made them only slightly less than divine, crowning them with glory and grandeur."

The keyword here is, '*slightly.*'

If we are *slightly* less than God Himself, then we are something. Unfortunately, religion has reduced us to worms, to sinners, to beings that have fallen short of the glory of God. King David, in his inspirational emendations, does not think so. He believes that we have been created a little lower than Elohim.

The ASV (American Standard Version) goes, "For thou hast made him but little lower than God, And *crownest* him with glory and honour." What a staggering unfathomable statement that is! I have taken my time to ponder it over, and I've still not been able to get to the end of it.

If the Great God has created us a little lower than Him, who are we then? I am very sure that we generally have, as mankind, disappointed. We have been dominated, we have been slaves, we have been subhuman, we have been worse than what God has destined us to be. Whether by circumstance or the mere colour of skin.

History tells us that we, whether black or white, brown or yellow, have not lived up to the expectations of the God who created and mandated us.

We are all the children of God, and we can do better, much better than we have done before. The man reciting the exultation of man in the above scriptures had done exploits in his life from as soon as he got this revelation. This is the famous bear killer, lion destroyer, giant slayer, the one who became King without been sired by royalty.

The world has always been large enough to be able to accommodate and sustain several empires. And empires are not only political entities like kingdoms. And when these sons of God play their game, *izinja ze game,* it is indeed a manifestation.

It is phenomenal, a spectacle to watch. I say unto you, 'You could become emperor of your own in your own domain or sphere of influence; you have been created for such things as those.' And this is what I am talking about when I am talking about, 'empire builders.'

These are daring players who carve their own path, who, in the words of the poet Robert Frost are willing to walk 'the road less travelled by.'

"You are your only competition because your gifts are only within you."

Moshe Rabbenu was not a fringe player. He was an empire builder. He gave us the Ten Commandments and is credited with writing the first five books of the Old Testament and founded the Jewish nation.

Simon Jose Antonio Bolivar was not on anybody's bench. He founded the nation of Bolivia. The Libertador led what are currently Venezuela, Bolivia, Colombia, Ecuador, Peru and Panama to independence from the Spanish Empire.

Kaizer Motaung of Soweto, where I was born and half raised, is not a fringe player. He built the international football brand called Kaizer Chiefs F.C.

Giorgio Armani of Italy built a clothing empire around himself, called by his name, and extended the brand to other fields.

Behind those empires was great passion. Without passion, you are a non-starter. Passion, what another writer called 'loving absorption', is a very important ingredient here. It is passion that will get you going when your vehicle runs out of gas, and it will happen a few times on your path, especially if you have high aims in life.

You could be the next leader of your own empire, largely influenced by your own understanding of global influence. Only in a positive way you were created to become a person of power and influence. Not that you would be competing with anybody else, but you ought to compete with yourself. You are your only competition because your gifts are only within you. Talking about gifts, it is indeed a tragedy to be born in this world and later depart without knowing what the divine power had implanted in you, because no one is ever born without that impartation.

You are required by your mandate by the Higher Power to influence change and make a lasting impact in your living years, and hopefully even after. All the names I have mentioned before have either outlived or will outlive their empires. If immortality shall indeed accrue to men, it will be to empire builders.

Your posture should be different as you walk the earth because you know why you are here. You should over and above all be present and genuinely involved in making a change in the world and in your lifetime.

Infuse passion into what you have decided to become, add to that diligence and relentlessness, and you are on your way to the place I am leading you to.

As in the story of the mustard seed, empires are not born huge, they are born small, and they enlarge themselves according to the vision and workings of the founder. If you infuse enthusiasm and passion to every idea you birth, there are no limits to how far you can go and how large you can build whatever you build.

Don't you just like the word founder? It is a grand designation to attach to your name - "Founder of...." You've got to aim to be the founder of something. You've got to intend to leave your name behind when you depart from these shores.

Even if we can live for another ten thousand years, there are names this world will never be able to erase from their memories. These are people who were able to buy immortality in their lifetimes. Their tomb inscriptions will not be blurred by time and the elements.

The poet Ben Johnson in his poem; "To The Memory of my Beloved, the Author Mr William Shakespeare", writes ending a very beautiful and memorable poem;

But stay, I see thee in the hemisphere
Advanc'd, and made a constellation there!
Shine forth, thou star of poets, and with rage
Or influence, chide or cheer the drooping stage;
Which, since thy flight from hence, hath mourn'd like night,
And despairs day, but for thy volume's light.

In his poem "Adonais: An elegy on the death of John Keats", Percy Bysshe Shelley writes,

I weep for Adonais—he is dead!
Oh, weep for Adonais! Though our tears
Thaw not the frost which binds so dear a head!
And thou, sad Hour, selected from all years
To mourn our loss, rouse thy obscure compeers,
And teach them thine own sorrow, say: "With me
Died Adonais; till the future dares
Forget the Past, his fate and fame shall be
An echo and a light unto eternity!"

And somewhere in the verse, he continues,

To that high Capital, where kingly Death
Keeps his pale court in beauty and decay,
He came; and bought, with price of purest breath,
A grave among the eternal.—

And John Keats, (31 October 1795 – 23 February 1821), who died at the tender age of 25, had already made a great impact in the world, as lamented and praised by a very successful poet himself, Shelley.

By the end of the century, Keats had been placed within the canon of English literature and had become the inspiration for the Pre-Raphaelite Brotherhood, with a strong influence on many writers.

The Pre-Raphaelite Brotherhood (later known as the Pre-Raphaelites) was a group of English painters, poets, and art critics, founded in 1848 by William Holman Hunt, John Everett Millais, Dante Gabriel Rossetti, William Michael Rossetti, James Collinson, Frederic George Stephens and Thomas Woolner. They formed a seven-member "Brotherhood" modelled in part on the Nazarene movement.

As for Mr William Shakespeare, he needs no introduction in any world where the English tongue is spoken and taught.

So empires, as you follow my drift, are not necessarily limited to physical entities. They could be made of anything; gifts, talents, expertise, and know how's. The substance that makes empires be they physical or non-physical, is something of the soul.

One important thing is that an empire builder needs to adapt and adjust himself to the times. Times, they are 'a changing' — All the time. We live in a fluid world.

Be alive to the fact that organisations all over the world are aligning their competitiveness, not only based on their bottom lines and profitability but how relevant they will be in addressing the future and things pertinent.

Things such as climate change, sustainability, environmental awareness, tripple bottom lines, which concepts did not exist during the industrial and capitalist revolutions, are now on the table and refuse to be ignored.

Empire builders do not only evolve the world, they also evolve with the world but mostly not leading from behind. Like dinosaurs, there are entire industries and product lines that have become extinct because they failed to adapt to the changing times and were rendered irrelevant. Empire builders thrive on innovation and more innovation. They continuously re-imagine their lives and their organisations.

Therefore, the world needs an empire builder that will provoke and inspire fresh and new ideas. - A leader that will bring something different to the table. Leadership means first, in other words, leadership is not just management but *pioneership*. A true leader inspires even people outside of his sphere. It does not matter what your talents are, talent inspires other talents. A musician can inspire an author, and an author can inspire business.

Who are you inspiring right now? A true leader inspires and influences more than an entire generation regardless of their crafts and callings.

Millions of our young people are out of school, out of work, poor, hungry and about to commit a crime. These social ills, as stated above, are somewhat disturbing and call for leadership and need to be remedied. Albeit, they can be overcome through inspirational leadership.

You may have been sidelined to the peripheries, but you don't have to allow it. Outgrow the sidelining by the very force of your will. Empires are explosive entities, they begin, they grow, and they explode – positive explosions, of course. They are the giant creatures of the world, the adapting dinosaurs of our age, whatever world they show themselves in.

The man who saved an island

Talking about being inspired? I was inspired by the story of a man who undertook to save his native island—Padmashree 'Molai' Jadav Payeng of India. Dreams deferred too early have a way of haunting aging souls, and this man Jadav, the man who saved an island by planting a forest in it, understood that adage.

The Molai Forest, named after him, is the world's largest and the wealthiest forest in Northeast India. Being a man-made forest, I find it even more fascinating. Thanks to the saving grace of one, Padmashree Jadav Payeng, who created this magic of life and is now widely revered as the 'forest man of India' for over 30 years now. He faithfully and meticulously undertook to save his island, creating a forest and restoring wildlife in it.

That is where he decided to build his empire, which is growing lofty and lush every day.

"Empire builders do not only evolve the world, they also evolve with the world..."

This is the man who single-handedly went to 'plant and tend trees along the Sandbar on the Majuli Island' to mitigate against soil erosion from the river that was eating up the land, eventually causing the flooding of human habitats.

Jadav's greatest drive to plant was his encounter with many dead snakes that he would find lying helplessly due to high temperatures.

Some sceptics would say to him when he started planting, 'what do you think you can do or mitigate against the mighty river?' He turned a deaf ear to them. In his mind, he thought, 'Well, 'if he planted every day for 38 years, he could achieve quite a lot in time."

In re-imagining and re-living the scenario, Jadav thought about time. He believed that it could be done if it is done one day at a time, as in little by little. He thought that if he was consistent in doing it day by day, one tree at a time, it could turn into a forest. It is said that his uncompromising consistency is the one that changed everything.

If a man is able to think or plan for 38 years, that man will be unstoppable. Little by little, over 38 years is a whole lot. There is nothing you cannot create with that kind of mentality. The world is full of short-term thinkers; please do not be found amongst those. Empire builders are long-term thinkers and usually avoid short-term gratifications. They postpone gratifications until their goals are reached.

'We all have our Majulis,' majestically echoed the Elder. 'We just need to tend them, restore them to their full strength so that they could bring peace and tranquillity to humanity.'

Our pursuits should not deviate us from 'planting', albeit, little by little.

Apart from that, Jadav has been recognised and has received world recognition through many awards he has won. Today the Molai forest houses Bengal tigers, Indian rhinoceros, reptiles, deers, and rabbits, in addition to monkeys and several varieties of birds, including a large number of vultures.

Talking about vultures, they have their purpose too, to clean the earth. It's just that they mostly do not wish the sick and ailing good health. That is the only problem I have with them. When ailing in the forest, they will never pray for your recovery. In that, vultures make very bad Christians.

We can all house great species of beings in the vast forests of our minds and fulfilled dreams, if we learn to focus a little. We too can become havens of hope for others.

Needless to say that Jadav began his miraculous journey at the age of 16. Coming from a *marginalised* tribe, he could have exempted himself and abandoned such a great mission, which has changed not the course of history for him but also for the many, including those elephants that make Molai a habitat. 'Dreams deferred too early, have a way of haunting souls.'

Regrettably, due to the demands of life, some have abandoned their islands, yet we should never abandon our missions, no matter the cost.

Man has created orchards and plantations, but who ever thought that a man can actually create a forest? Men of tenacity and relentlessness, empire builders, can create almost anything. With such men, all things are possible because they believe.

3 OCCUPYING YOUR SPACE

Finding Your Niche

The most creative act you will ever undertake is the act of creating yourself. - **Deepak Chopra**

Finding your space in life can be hard at the beginning, but it shouldn't be. 'Who am I?' and 'What am I here for' are very challenging questions to ask oneself, yet very critical, perhaps even intriguing if life is an intrigue, which I believe it is.

During the 13th Century, one of Rabbi Meir of Rothenburg's disciples was Mordechai ben Hillel, who became one of the astute sages who today in the Jewish faith is regarded as one of the wisest men in the ilk of King Solomon. He began with humble means, a noble mission and a breathtaking vision that propelled the Jewish civilisation into a new generation of achievers. By the looks of things, his mission truly liberated a whole nation and not just a generation.

In his famous adage, 'if I am not for myself, who will be for me?' Hillel presents 'a hierarchy of responsibilities, in which our commitment to ourselves needs to be primary, yet not singular.' And so, in the discourse of growth, personal mastery enables one to appreciate that you can't give what you don't have. Therefore the paramount responsibility to yourself is to *institutionalise* your mission and calibrate it into your value system first so that when you serve others, you are aligned with your true purpose. Then your service to humanity will not be in vain, irrespective of the station you occupy in life.

Hillel further retorted that one's current relationship with self-care is essential as we advance. So, how do you want it to look like? What is one small step you can take towards developing a practice of self-care? Even before you undertake a journey to 'save' the world, save yourself first.

Be kind to yourself and remind yourself that you have been placed by life into a position of significance. Therefore you cannot waste yourself. Self-preservation leads to a strong sense of mission and direction.

One of the most challenging things growing up for me was finding my space in life, bringing my ship into the breeze, that is. So, if you would allow me, I would like to call it space-crafting?

I saw people who were, in my opinion, in their spaces, who were milking the legendary IT, and making strides in the world. They came out of the same abyss of apartheid and forced-removals like everyone else. I saw these special people everywhere and elsewhere in the country wherever I treaded my uncertain feet, and I wanted to find out their secret.

Were they lucky or foreordained to succeed and achieve greatness? Were they *behung* with the gold of favour from their mother's wombs? Why were they making it and not everybody else? At that time, I was part of everybody else, and I wanted out of it.

What made these people tick? Their greatness was of course exaggerated by common consent. But I knew that upon closer inspection, I could fathom their secret. The luxuries they enjoyed needed little endorsement of speech.

What made them different and set them apart from all the others, from us, the '*everybodys*'? These people just dazzled me from the pure *lustre* of their light, and there was birthed in my soul a desire to be one amongst them.

As I said earlier, my father was aware of all those people and admired them dearly and wanted me to do so. 'See them and admire them' seemed to be what my father wanted for me. In that, he was perhaps one of my greatest teachers.

It was like him saying, I missed the plane, but son, I will not let you miss it too. So he talked me through the exhibition, and he found inclined ears. I believe hc was God's sophistical whisper in my childish ear, and I was his little disciple.

At that time, the desire to make it in this world was injected into the labyrinth of my arteries. Thus, even though we are born with a positive outlook, the vicissitudes of this life demand that positivity needs to be cultivated regularly.

As I went through mansion by mansion, business centre by business centre, my eyes stood out of my head when I beheld the marvels and splendours. For a minute and sundry odd seconds, I lived their lives in the temple of my imagination.

These were not idle men. They had found their spaces and worked them. Yet, at the same time, their fellow villagers in the lump, mingled and revelled in their cities' fun and frolic, their forces sundered by the belief that they had been successfully reduced to nothingness by the ruling hegemony.

I am sure that other people beheld the beauty that was being exhibited to me, but mostly with vacant and worshipful admiration.

Meaningfully admiring the success and greatness of others does not seem like a step on the ladder, but it is because, whether we like it or not, admiring is aspiring and aspiring is a force on its own. Evan Esar says, "Success is the good fortune that comes from aspiration, desperation, perspiration and inspiration."

As I observed this exhibition, the question in my mind was, 'What made these people find and push into those spaces, their spaces? The idea of finding and pushing go together in this regard. But the keyword here is spaces, spaces, spaces! These men grew heavy with increase and stately possessions while their neighbours were simply eking out a living.

By spaces, I am also referring to what in business *lingo* is called niches. Or areas of expertise and focus.

Richard Maponya's niche was the retail business. It was very difficult for most people to compete with him in that space in the full tide of his strength and instincts.

Of course, he later expanded into other fields.

Kaizer Motaung's niche was football entrepreneurship and

management, and even today, he hardly has a rival in this country, even on the continent. And I am not saying that his team is winning every trophy. I am just saying that in that niche, he is the Kaiser. But, of course, he also expanded into other fields too.

Like many other questions about what makes people successful, one must also ask, among other things, the questions, "How do you find your area of expertise or niche? What fields best suit your personality, traits and skills." And these questions must be asked and answered firmly, honestly and fearlessly.

Nobody who has ever lived a worthy life has ever escaped the answering of these questions. The answers of which are the telescope into the future you want and desire. These questions are both spiritual and material, with consequences and ramifications. You have to pass that examination to get somewhere and become somebody in this life, happy, healthy, wealthy, and much more.

"Institutionalise your mission and calibrate it into your value system."

In this country, there is a great emphasis on passing the twelfth grade, otherwise known as matric. Personally, I think compared to the questions I have mentioned above, passing matric is a rather pale object. And by so saying, I am not suggesting that matric is not important. However, it would be best if you still had it to enter into university and certain jobs and opportunities.

One of the most intriguing and impactful persons who ever lived by all standards, Jesus Christ of Nazareth's famous sayings was what theologians have dubbed His 'I am' sayings.'

These are amongst the phrases that fitfully annoyed the Pharisees, the Sadducees and the so-called Scribes of His days. You could say that he knew who he was and expressed it with crystal clarity and fearlessness while being watched with the fierce and murderous red eyes of religious fanatics and fundamentalists.

"I am the bread of life," he said to a hungry crowd.

"I am the way the truth and the life and nobody goes to the Father except through me," to a spiritually lost multitude.

"I am the light of the world, he who follows Me shall not walk in darkness, but have the light of life", to a community in the throes of darkness

"I am the Door." (John 10:9)

"I am the Good Shepherd."(John 10:11,14)

"I am the Resurrection and the Life."(John 11:25)

"I am the Vine."(John 15:1,5)

I am, I am, I am.

Now, who are you?

It mostly sounded arrogant, though, but it was his self-knowledge that he was expressing.

I know that some of the things he said, his 'I am' sayings, might be contestable across other cultures and religions, but I am sure my point is made.

There is no need to contest a man, any man's "*I am's*." It is your "*I am's*" that are important. Who are you? Answer that question, and it will make the most significant difference in your life.

People of impact are people of un-debatable self-knowledge. And un-debatable in this sense is that they are unwilling to debate with anybody else about who they are.

So why should you discuss such a vital question and have an altercation with the world about it? Why should there be another party in you tackling such an essential issue in life? Why do you want to give other people such a franchise in your life? And the true "I am's" are rather staggering and could be misconstrued and unbearable to others. But, of course, this does not mean that you should necessarily utter them in public.

When Muhammad Ali said, "I am the greatest", the world dropped its jaw. Today if you ask people who in the field of boxing was the greatest ever, there is very little debate about the answer to the question.

Likewise, you must find your "I am's" Who are you or who do you think you are? These questions are critical to your success, happiness and fulfilment in this life. Such questions can be perplexing as you grow and yet beautiful when you find the answers because that is when you find your magic. Whether the world contests your "I am's" or not is immaterial; as long as you own up to them, they will work for you.

REMEMBER, "KNOW THYSELF."

In my measured opinion, this was supposed to be the foundational teachings of the school system. As I told you earlier, a friend of mine told me that the person who founded the modern school system was a Frankenstein, an evil genius. I asked him why and he said, "The person who created the modern schooling system left out all the most important elements, and I think it's because he wanted to control the world." I am still trying to contemplate that because the man who told me this is a brilliant man. Where I am concerned, everything called education must begin there or nowhere else.

"I AM THAT I AM" is supposed to be the liquid name of God. That is what YAHWEH or Jehovah in English means. It should be the liquid name of any man who wants to be a person of substance— no less. You have got to be an 'I am' to become something or somebody. To be unable to answer the question 'Who am I?' is a very tragic position to be in life.

Yet many people drift through this existence clueless about that fundamental. Yet, on the other hand, some of the most successful people I have known knew very early in their lives who they were and what they wanted to make out of their lives. So foundational education should address that, and the teachers at that level of education should ideally be trained in child psychology and psychology at large.

In his book, 'The Present', Spencer Johnson engages a beautiful story of a young lad who undertakes a journey into adulthood and is about to receive a gift from an old man. He despises and rejects the gift.

Later in his life, the young man crawls back with his tail between his legs to ask the older man about the gift he despised when he was young.

The old man, with that hoarse voice admonishing him, 'only you have the power to find The Present for yourself.'

'And so the young man embarks on a tireless search for this magical gift that holds the secret to his personal happiness and wealth.'

It was after a great search, having gone and experienced the 'four winds of the earth', that he discovers The Present, the very moment he was in. The present, the current vibration of your heart, the breathing and the pulsing—that is your gift from God. It is truly a rare blessing to own that moment. So breathe in, sip that coffee and be grateful about what life has to offer.

"Savour the moment and live a life of grand discovery."

Another thing, never stop producing your craft, and in all fairness, that is what should *pre-occupy* you. Trust your craft and trust the process that it will yield glorious moments for you.

Breaking this down intellectually, I am saying that life is lived in the moment, that today is the only guaranteed moment, and that breathing the air is the greatest opportunity of all. And breathe it not in asthmatic spasms; breathe it with grateful ease for it is the gift of God.

We worry so much about tomorrow and regret so much about yesterday that we miss the moment - the present. But, as we advance in life, we realise that life can only be lived in the present. You can't live yesterday, and you can't live tomorrow no matter how hard you try. The only gift from the universe for you is the present moment.

One of Dale Carnegie's principles for overcoming worry is to live in "day-tight compartments." This term was first coined by Sir William Osler when he encountered this life-changing quote from Thomas Carlyle, "It is not our goal to see what lies dimly in the distance but to do what lies clearly at hand."

In your living years, continue, consistently creating mastery around yourself and your gifts. It is better that you produce little but everlasting masterpieces.

Rhonda Bryne, in her ubiquitous book the Greatest Secret, further escalates the notion of self-mastery, and she writes that "when you fully recognise who you are, you will have a life without problems, without upsets, hurts or worries. You will be free from the life of fear and death and will never again be controlled by or tortured by your mind." She continues, "Further ideas and beliefs will dissolve. In their place will be clarity, happiness, joy, peace, infinite fun and wonder – every moment a delight. You will know you are safe and secure, no matter what."

Gary Zukav expressed it beautifully in his book "The Seat of the Soul" that when you find an alignment in your life where your soul is in sync with your purpose, authentic power is inevitable. The reason we live and move and have our being is to fulfil that pursuit. This intrinsic power causes us to live gainful lives." He (Gary) concludes by saying, "when we align our thoughts, emotions, and actions with the highest part of ourselves, we are filled with enthusiasm, purpose and meaning." At this level of prowess, fear can visit but never conquer your soul. You become unstoppable.

It is therefore possible to halt your life's bankruptcy and emptiness if it has gotten to that. Life can still blossom at any time of your existence on earth. All these hinge upon how you carry your emotions, how you cherish your dreams, and how you deliver on your destiny.

The superlatives of humans lie in our intrinsic nature of nobility. It was in 1849 when Alice Cary, in her great work of poetry entitled, "Nobility", that she made a stark observation that "true worth is in being, not seeming, in doing, each day that goes by, some little good – not dreaming."

So investing in your life may be the most significant achievement that yields happiness and continuous joy. Being fully present and genuinely engaged in building your life up and the lives of those around you could be the most altruistic form of personal mastery.

All you need is to develop the capacity to handle your next level of inner peace until you are content with yourself. Then, depart from and shun mediocrity in all its formations and refuse to over-produce non-essentials.

Be fixated on living to your best creed, your great calling and live 'the present.' It's a gift to you from the Higher Power; embrace it.

4 LET THERE BE LIGHT

The First Step of Creation

Do it right the first time is insane advice. Nobody does anything INTERESTING right the first or the twenty-first, or the forty-first time. Doing the new means screwing around, trying stuff, and messing stuff up. That is WASTE. So how's your WQ., Waste Quotient? (No kidding!) - **Tom Peters**

Desire is the first step of creation. Desiring (present continuous) is the second step. Asking is the third step. It also doesn't matter whether you ask man, God, the universe, or yourself. '*Intention*' is the next step, and attention follows after that.

In the book "The Vortex" by Esther and Jerry Hicks, they assert that beginning is the first step in the creation process. As much as I agree with many things the book preaches, I disagree with that one assertion.

Beginning, the doing or starting to do something is a very fragile process. If there ever was a devil, he lives just a few miles from where it all begins. This is the snake in the path or the grass for all creators, but then when he opens his eyes and mind, there are also ladders. Always! It's a game — snakes and ladders.

The question is, are you going to concentrate on the snakes or on the ladders? Will you focus on what takes you down or what brings you up into a place of permissive allowance?

Many things fail at the beginning; it is the willingness to try again even what has failed at the beginning that has sustained all things we call successful. And this is if the desire is strong enough, even stronger than what might happen against it. So if we acknowledge that there are snakes as much as there are ladders, then we should agree with my assertion.

"Be mindful of the actions that will follow your first attempts at anything."

Not many people have succeeded at first thrust. In reading biographies, and I have read a lot of those, I hardly remember anybody who did. The first day of creation, even with God, was horrible. That is when 'the world was without form and void, and darkness was upon the face of the deep.'

The first of God's creatures—'light,' did the worst that could happen to any creator. She exposed the disaster. So on day one, all God saw was sewerage, and he had to go into day two, if he wasn't God, depressed. In a paradoxical way of speaking, day two is the real day one of creation, any creation.

In other words, day two is perhaps the more important day of creation. When we were babies, we walked on day one and on that day, on the first step, we fell on our little butts, but we stood up and tried again. So as you walk the earth with long strides and confidence, remember that you failed in your first, second, third, and I don't know how many attempts else, no matter who you are.

Day two is important because it is the day of the champions. It is the day that says that those who try once have no chance for success in this world. Day two is the little that comes after the first little. Day two means that you are aware of the necessity of the second step, and if you are aware of that, you will be mindful of the action that will follow that. And that is to me what little by little means.

I am talking about creation at this stage because born of God; we are all born with creative forces and energies within. God created a forest, the fauna and the flora, and then he left the rest to us to continue with what he started.

The beautiful landscapes, *city-scapes*, pyramids and obelisks, and all the creations that adorn the earth are the creations of man, made in the image of God.

Sometimes, you should take time to travel or look up these big cities, New York, Los Angeles, Dubai, Sandton, and Kuala Lampur. Oh! What majestic buildings adorn those cities. Today with online technology, you can even see the seven wonders of the earth while in the comfort of your home in 4D. These are new worlds made by man.

These are God's delights because I am sure as a Father, he delights in the exploits of his children. While touring the world, I met a man wearing a Kaizer Chiefs T-shirt who was not even from Africa, never mind South Africa, and I said, wow!

It would help if you endeavoured to be one of those whose creations, in whatever form, adorn the earth. But, there is no reason why you should exclude yourself from that ilk.

Those who find themselves excluded from that splendour are self-excluding. Only you can exclude yourself in this world because just by your mere birth and the miracle of it all, you are included.

I say this because even during the days of slavery in America, there were still slaves, bondmen and women who did exploits and created great things with or without patents. They were saying to history; slavery excluded us, but we refuse to exclude ourselves.

That, right there, is the creed of all creators.

Slave owners often took credit for their slaves' inventions because of envy, and because they thought owned the slaves, they believed they also owned whatever invention they created.

In one well-documented case, a black inventor named Ned invented an effective, innovative cotton scraper. His slave master, Oscar Stewart, attempted to patent the invention, however, because Stewart was not the actual inventor, the application was rejected because the true inventor was born into slavery.

Benjamin Montgomery, born into slavery, invented in 1819 a steamboat propeller designed for shallow waters. This was a valuable invention as it facilitated the delivery of food and critical items. Free blacks sometimes did successfully receive patents. One example is Thomas Jennings, the first black patent holder, who invented dry-cleaning in 1821.

Philanthropist and entrepreneur Madam C.J. Walker (real name Sarah Breedlove) invented an innovative line of African American hair care products in 1905 that led to her distinction as one of America's first self-made millionaires. After almost one hundred and thirty years, her highly successful cosmetics company is still in business today.

Anyone who's ridden modern elevators has Alexander Miles to thank for the stair alternative's automatic doors.

These are too numerous to enumerate. And my point here is not to usher you into the space of 'Black History Month.'

I am not talking black, I am talking creation against all odds.

I am simply making the point that those who think that they are excluded are self-excluding. Period!

According to the Thesaurus, little by little also means gradually, by small degrees or amounts, fitfully, fragmentary.

Gradually!

Shinku's poem, "*Little by little*", is one inspirational piece of kindergarten verse, and it reads as follows:

"Little by little," an acorn said,
As it slowly sank in its mossy bed;
"I am improving every day,
Hidden deep in the earth away."
Little by little, each day it grew,
Little by little, it seeped the dew.

Downward it sent a thread-like root
Up in the air sprang a tiny shoot;
Day by day, and year by year,
Little by little, the leaves appear,
And the slender branches spread far and wide.
Till the mighty oak is the forest's pride.

Far down in the depths of the dark blue sea,
An insect train works ceaselessly.
Grain by grain, they are building well,
Each one alone in its little cell.

Moment by moment, and day by day,
Never stopping to rest or play,
Rocks upon rocks, they are rearing high,
Till the top looks out on the sunny sky.
The gentle wind and the balmy air,
Little by little, bring verdure there;
Till the summer sunbeams gaily smile
On the buds and the flowers of the coral isle.

"Little by little," said a thoughtful boy,
"Moment by moment, I'll employ,
Learning a little every day,
And not spending all my time in play.
And still, this rule in my mind shall dwell,
Whatever I do, I will do it well.

"Little by little, I'll learn to know
The treasured wisdom of long ago;
And one of these days, perhaps we'll see
That the world will be the better for me,"
And do you not think that this simple plan
Made him a wise and useful man?

Little by little is a very beautiful and illustrious poem but what is very telling and significant about it is that it demonstrates the relentlessness and the necessary diligence behind the philosophy.

Little by little is not a laid-back philosophy where one sits back and watches the world slowly drift by and hope that it will drift with them like a river would, to drift-wood. It is an active philosophy, a philosophy of doing.

Christ used to command incapacitated people, "Rise up and walk." In other words, 'even though I have the miracle power to heal you, I demand of you to do something active yourself.' They could have easily asked, "how do I rise up and walk when I have not been able to do that for the last 38 years? Are you kidding me?"

I remember an intriguing story about twelve lepers who stood by the gate of Bethany. Leprosy being an infectious disease, lepers were not allowed to mingle with healthy society. They had to isolate themselves somewhere amongst like people. When they heard that Jesus was to pass by their vicinage, and they saw the crowd milling around him and moving with him, they were whelmed by the occasion and started shouting, 'Jesus son of David, have mercy on us.'

How they got to hear about this healer, we must give credit to the fellow with a thousand tongues — '*rumour*.'

Think about a forlorn people whom society had ostracised to the periphery. Pretty much waiting for their death or a miracle, and miracles happened far and apart.

People, whom it was dangerous and deadly to associate with, yet somebody loved one of them enough to risk their life and tell them of a man who healed people, whose name was Jesus.

"Little by little is an active philosophy that moves you from dream to achievement."

It was like, "Hey Cuz, I know you are stricken and hopeless, but there is a new healer and prophet in town called Jesus. He hails from Nazareth, and he is going to pass this way on such a day, make sure you scream and shout, and if he hears you, he will certainly heal you. So he whispered this hope to the others.

He must have told them what his cousin had told him. I am sure there were sceptics amongst them as there always are in every society. But out of sheer desperation, they held on to that word. When Jesus and his crew passed by that place, the one who had been briefed knew what to do, and his fellows joined him. They screamed and shouted like they had never shouted before and said, 'Jesus son of David, have mercy on us.'

The crowd insulated him from being heard.

They could have stopped right there and said that he had not heard them. But they desired the healing so badly and believed that the man Jesus had healing for them, so they shouted even louder. 'Jesus, son of David, have mercy on us.' Jesus heard them, and He said unto them, "Go and shew yourself to the priests."

By the Law of Moses, if a leper got healed by some miracle, he would have to go to the priests for certification that he was healed and then be allowed back to healthy society.

And what did Christ say to those lepers? He said, "Go and show yourself to the priests." In other words, by that decree, I am healing you. And as one preacher beautifully put it, 'and as they *goed* (as in went), they were healed. If they had sat down there and said, 'if we go to the priests, people who might meet us on the way would stone us,' (for that was the Law), they would have never gotten their cleansing.

It was in the act of believing and going that their healing manifested. If they had sat there and moaned and said to themselves, "how do we show ourselves to the priests in this condition?" They would have been stoned for breaking the law of Moses.

At that moment, they would have remained in their condition, and Jesus would have marched to the next town to deal with those that were willing to believe him and act on his command.

Little by little, they walked to the temple of examination and certification because they believed. I am saying to you today that the temple of healing is a couple of steps away, but you have to walk the walk of faith. It is not and never going to happen while you sit down and analyse. Little by little is an active philosophy that moves you from dream state to a *state* of achievement.

Understanding the big picture, and knowing how the little pieces fall into place gives one a sense of direction. As a farmer would know, there is seed time, growing time, weeding time, pruning time and harvest time. In between all of these, there is time.

When you look at a building construction, when it is complete, all that one sees is the beauty and splendour of creation, what they don't sees is the wiring that runs between the walls, the not so good looking bricks and plaster before the coat painting. Little by little is the insight into the many pieces that come together to form a whole.

Every single day, you are a work in progress, a creation in the process. The words "Let there be light,...: give permission of creation to proceed, continuously, indefinitely into all of existence. Give yourself and the world around you permission to "Let there be...". ∎

5 SELF DISCOVERY

Finding Your Sacred Place

In the beginning, there was nothing. God said, 'Let there be light!' And there was light. There was still nothing, but you could see it a whole lot better. - **Ellen DeGeneres**

Enlightenment is a big word in spirituality. I know that it is not a very popular word in the Christian faith, but the truth is, being the children of the light as you are, 'the light of the world,' Christians should not shirk away from such a beautiful concept.

Enlightenment is *awareness*, and it is the coming into the light. At best, it is even becoming the '*light of the world*' as Christ once preached. But enlightenment is not the preserve of any religious group or religious people. It is the preserve of all mankind

Most of humanity that is not in with this kind of programme is in a state of slumber. Most of the world's people are wearing pyjamas every day and snoring at one another, confusing that for conversation. Yet, all the great truths in the world brought to us were by people who transcended this sphere into the next. In a manner of speaking, those transcendent individuals were enlightened.

I live in a country that was dominated by colonists, white people, and every time I park my car in the city, there is a black person who calls me *umlungu*, which directly translates to 'white man' in many of the Nguni languages of Southen Africa.

As black I am, I am often taken aback when another person of my skin colour refers to me as '*umlungu*', even in my darkened skin. It does not matter how often I rebuke this tendency; it remains the same from one corner of town to the other and from one town to another. '*Mlungu wam*,' '*lekgowa la ka*' in the other popular tongue; annoys me very much.

"Possibility is available to us when we are connected to the sources of creation."

If my people call me that, what do they call the white people, gods? Could they be groping and going down on their knees when they see white people? So in my country, there are black people who think that the White man is the better man, and the Black person who drives a car and can throw you a few pennies is elevated to become a white man.

It pains me badly because I think it is unnatural. This *down-trodden-ness* bothers me a whole lot—this '*beggarliness*,' this elevation of others, whether black or white, is *unhuman* and ungodly. I can understand the many years of positioning that the white race has had globally, but we are humanity, and it should only take a few lessons to uplift oneself to that place of origin.

We answer to only one Deity, and we are a little lower than the Almighty according to his word, black or white. Why should we lower ourselves to others, any others? Man is supposed to think highly of himself without being haughty no matter what his material conditions are. Man is also supposed to consider himself equal to others no matter how humble his condition. We are not, by any stretch of the imagination, our material condition. We are a lot more than that.

When Joseph went into Egypt through strange circumstances, he went there as a sold slave, a commodity. But he never allowed himself to drift down to that condition. He was taken to prison on false accusations but was never a prisoner. You could not imprison such a soul. He ended up the Prime Minister to the Pharaoh, ruler of that once most powerful land, Egypt.

Joseph was such a young star, a dreamer who went out there to demonstrate greater powers and literally pulled a nation out of its economic crisis. He was the first man in Bible times to restructure a national fiscus, reposition Egyptian National Debt and brought much relief and prosperity for everyone. It is evident when you read the story of Joseph that he lived in a different realm than the commoner. He was an enlightened soul who, even in his sleep, was able to walk on clouds. He soared above whatever circumstance that was thrown at him. Man is supposed to be able to live above his circumstances, any circumstance.

That possibility is available to us. Lots of histories and biographies can attest to that. But, if you can check their stories, the greatest amongst us did not necessarily have it that easy. It was not '*ease*' that fashioned their greatness.

More than anything else, it was the difficulties. But one thing very clear is that they seemed to be hearing the sound of a distant drummer nobody could hear.

No great man answers to the name of greatness who has not had to fight the lions and bears of the wilderness which this world can sometimes turn in. That kind of greatness is incomplete and leaves no lessons behind.

BEING ONE WITH NATURE

When man was first fashioned, God plunged him into a place amongst nature. He was surrounded by the fauna and the flora. Man's first teacher was God Himself. His second teacher was nature. Also, the Bible has never undermined nature in its expressions.

Remember that nature was physically here on planet earth before man. What makes you aware that there is something extraordinary in nature is the biblical allegories, the anecdotes, the teachings, the similes and the metaphors about nature.

Henry David Thoreau wrote in his memoirs, "I once had a sparrow alight upon my shoulder for a moment, while I was hoeing in a village garden, and I felt that I was more distinguished by that circumstance than I should have been by any epaulette I could have worn."

One of Christ's greatest sermons was "look at the birds of the air, ... the lilies of the field." He taught us to look at nature and learn. King Solomon himself had also earlier on directed us to that space when he said, "*look at the ants, thou sluggard.*"

That is because nature is God uninterrupted. Nature teaches us what God can do if not interrupted by human thought and action because nature does not think. It comes to be that what we thought was our greatest asset – to think, might just be our greatest liability if not used appropriately. If we did not think, I am sure that we could be angels. God made us thinking beings, a higher office than that of angels, a higher state of being.

We are the only creatures that can determine who they become. And both fortunately and unfortunately, it seems like God has no intention of interfering with that.

God hardly ever interferes with that; it's called free will. Adam could eat the forbidden fruit without God stopping him or striking him with lightning. We are the only beings whose future is entirely in our hands.

Nature is instinctive, and that is why it does not fail to be. We, more than any other beings created by God, have the ability to create ourselves and decide our destiny. This is delightful as much as it is burdensome.

With this introduction, let me travel with you to another thought –being one with nature. According to me, being one with nature is the highest form of enlightenment.

Talking about nature, I should perhaps get to the subject of rain. Rain is significant and unique because when God created the earth, there had been nothing called rain. Rain came later than creation. It was brought down to earth to enliven creation. Water is the greatest liquid of all, even greater than oil. In the beginning, both the fauna and the flora were thirsty. The earth thirsted for the greatest liquid.

Your rain must find you ready. "No plants were growing anywhere." God had not sent any rain, and there was no one to work the land." God had called for the light (Gen 1), but He had not called for the rain, and everything was ready to die.

As I sit to write, which is a routine that I have become accustomed to, even to love, I am doing it lovingly in the rain with its sound providing me with background music, if I might call it that. I love rain. That it was created after the earth just makes it so special to me. The rain is beautifully dripping down to earth, kissing the vegetation to bloom here in Polokwane and, I am very sure, elsewhere in the world.

Pula! Rain.

It is so effortlessly natural, and that's all it does, nurturing.

It's almost like by every drop, it is cheering up every dry leaf to live again and every unborn bud to show itself up as in, to live. According to me, rain was simply the final miracle of creation.

The Holy Book does not disagree because it speaks so much of rain, 'the former rain' and the 'latter rain', concepts amongst the greater biblical concepts is this agreement. But without going into the profundity of holy texts, I am in Polokwane right now in my study and listening to the sound of the rain, which is a very beautiful sound.

Rain is sent to all, yet those who are ready will use it gainfully to plant and water their fields into orchards of opportunities.

Those who understand its value will be the only beneficiaries; the rest will just get wet.

I have met a lot of wet people cursing the rainfall that happened *upon* them all because they were never ready for the *life-giving* waters.

When you are there to work the land, let the rain water those seeds and let them germinate and bear fruit and fruits that would remain. In places where rain falls, it is given to every person; equally. It is an equalizer, just like time. Some people use it better than others, which is what makes the difference between a man and his neighbour.

In ancient agrarian communities and economies, all they had was rain and the ground and soils they trod upon, but some people were poorer and others richer, even though the rain fell upon them equally on the self-same soils. How do you explain that? We are allocated the same time, and we have the same rain falling upon our heads and crops, but some succeed, and others fail.

The principles I want to share in this book are bent on making sure that you are not one of those who fail. It is not necessarily who you know that makes you successful.

I am afraid I have to disagree with that premise.

I believe what you know is much more important because what you know can bring you to people that are important, the "who you know" of this world. And the reason why I would write a book like this is to increase what you know about life, about health, about wealth and success in the main.

Remember that I am not saying that who you know is not important. I argue that the assertions, "what you know and who you know", have been lopsided to whom you know, and I vehemently disagree with that lopsidedness.

King Solomon said that your gift will bring you before great men. In other words, what you've got will take you somewhere. What you have or what you know will ultimately determine who you know and not the other way around. In other words, what you know is the highway to who you will know.

"Never underestimate the power of the planted seed."

As we continue talking about nature and being one with it, one aspect or creature in nature that is amazing must be a seed. Seeds are very potent things.

Christ talked about the mustard seed when he was teaching about faith. He also taught an agrarian community about a farmer who went out to plant seeds, and some of them fell on bad ground while the others fell on good ground. So the whole idea of planting seeds was to him a great metaphor of life - that in life, we plant seeds and reap the benefits or the consequences.

If you approach life with the respect of the cliché adage that 'in life, you reap what you sow', you will be progressive. This principle is as rigid as the gravitational force of the earth. It does not enter into negotiations with anyone. It simply is. And challenging it creates resistance in your life. If you jump of a building, gravity doesn't ask if you would like to go up or down. As the same applies to the principle of sowing and reaping. You cannot plant oranges and expect to reap bananas.

You will find yourself in a place where you blame no one, but the sower, which is, in all regards, your own self.

So keep planting, and keep watering the seeds that you've planted. The beauty with the seed is that once it is planted and then watered, it begins with its mission immediately, with its first goal being only to sprout. And how does the acorn become an oak? Little by little. I have yet to see a seed that looks alive in seed-form, but let it sprout, and you will know that things are not as they seem. Lifeless as they seem, seeds have a life of their own.

Therefore, it is prudent that you plant the right ones so that in the fullness of time, 'you reap what you've sown' becomes a delightful statement to yourself.

If you sow thorns and thistles, that is what you will reap, dear reader? So at the planting season, be awake to the fact that what you shall reap is what you would have sown. Always pay thorough attention to your seeds before you *sow* them. Be aware that sowing time is much more important than reaping time.

When the rain finds you ready, great shall be your harvest. The divine outpouring of blessings in anyone's life always has lasting benefits. God has sent rain to your field for your divine favour and a blessing, or I should rather say that God will.

You don't need to try hard, be effortless like rain, let God water your seeds, but for God's sake, plant something. If you plant nothing, even if the rain comes pouring down in torrents, what would your expectations be?

Never let your grain fields run dry. Instead, pray for and receive rain when it drops down. Ask God for rain, if anything.

Ask Him not for food, but rain for your crops, for the seeds you have planted because you are a working man or a woman.

The first man created was not born to leisure even though his world looked like a holiday paradise. He had a job from day one. He was to tend the land. Leisure is a beautiful thing, don't get me wrong, but if it were to become the routine of your life, you would hate the whole idea of living. I do not know how being a tramp feels like, but I am sure it is the worst terrible state of being.

Be like a blessed man who is 'like a tree planted by the rivers of water, that is evergreen in all seasons and whose leaf never withers. And whatever he does, he prospers.' Life is not just about breathing; it is about doing. Whatever he does, prospers - talks to that. So be a doing man or woman.

Rain is a symbol of being blessed, the state of being propelled to prosper even where others fail. It is this divine impartation of being made fruitful that just excites me. When you pace yourself to thrive like rain, you fill the earth with your ideas and your creations.

So God created the Heavens and the Earth as we now know them. There were plants everywhere, but no plants were growing anywhere. Two things were missing. One, God had not sent any rain and two, there was no one to work the land.

The lack of divine blessing dwarfs human progress. You will need to be connected to a Higher Power for your fields to be watered. It would be best if you also were ready when rain falls. You are the man who must work the land, whatever land is your domain, and if you ask God correctly, rain is guaranteed. If you plant the right seed, then you will get the right kind of harvest.

The Holy Book says, in one of the most profound statements, "While the earth *remaineth*, *seedtime* and harvest... shall not cease." Therefore, those who do not *seed* should not expect a harvest no matter how much they pray. That is principle.

It is incredible that in these changing times, some of the wealthiest people in this country, even in the world at large, are still farmers. I guess it's because we wake up hungry, and we all hate to go to bed hungry. But the lessons of seedtime and harvest and reaping what you sow are more profound.

There is an oasis of abundance that the Creator of the Universe leads us to after every rain drop. We all deserve a wonderful life, our own Nirvanas, our place of perfect peace and happiness, like heaven on earth. The highest state that you can attain, a product of the state of enlightenment.

After the rain, plant, till and cultivate your land with your own hands. Even though I talk about a heaven on earth, I do not mean to say that there will be no challenges. Your life doesn't have to be all 'whistles and bells' or performances of epic proportions, sometimes just being you and blissful is enough. If you can be enlightened to the idea that your life was blessed at birth, then your unique value will show.

What you don't need in your life is drought.

That aside, I want you to be the hero of your history, defying limitations that might try to hinder you. Let there be newness in your life, new beginnings that would make a considerable contribution to the lives of others. Let the God of the Universe place you into the genesis of your journey.

"Then I will send rain on your land in its season or both autumn rain and spring rains so that you may gather grain, new wine and olives," says the Lord in the holy writ — Deuteronomy 11:14.

Of all prayers, ever pray, "give us this day our daily bread", but at a higher level, ask God for rain because rain is the language of abundance. If God gives you rain, you may not have to ask for daily bread because it is right there in the rain. Every little drop of rain is prosperity. It is way more than bread.

"What is man, that You are mindful of him"

The world is a formidable structure ever since God created it. To change it, you will need another formidable force. The world was created by faith, and the force that will recreate the world is the very same force. The Bible says that without faith, it is impossible to please God.

When the Psalmist says in Psalm 8, "...when I consider the heavens, the work of thy fingers," he is saying something profound because we know that God created the heavens with his words, so the poet or Psalmist if you may, calls God's words fingers. How powerful are words? Powerful are words in God's mouth, and powerful are the words in this creature created in His image and after His likeness.

If humans were not thick-skulled, we could have created more planets ourselves. I am very sure that the statement that "God rested after six days of creation" was for Him to give a chance, a creative chance to His greatest creation to continue with the act and art of creation. I don't think he rested because He was tired. I don't imagine such a being, such an energy being fatigued.

When he rested, I think he wanted the crown of his creation, mankind, to take over because he created him to be capable of doing so. We are more capable than we think. We are so capacitated that if we awaken to our native powers, we would surprise ourselves. Unless words are just being flung around in the Holy Book, "let us create man in our image and after our own likeness" is huge. This is even larger when you know who God is. We, as human beings, need to awaken to God's expectation of us, but we have first to find our greatness.

If we are His children, his sons and daughters, I am very sure that He could be very disappointed with us in the main.

We, in religious circles, have concentrated on, "All have sinned and come short of the glory of God", instead of "...what is man that Thou are mindful of him and the son of man that Thou visitest him. You have made him a little lower than God..."

And that could just be me protecting God, which is very unnecessary. If you consider the heavens, that is, galaxies of which the milky way you know is not even one of the largest, "the works of thy fingers, what is man, that You are mindful of him" is a big statement. "... and the son of man that Thou visitest him." I like visitors a whole lot. But just imagine being visited by God Himself.

King David was not just being poetic; he was talking or writing from personal experience. Indeed God does visit humans. I can personally vouch for that. This galactic Creator of the universe is mindful of you. You must consider that the Bible was written before Galileo Galilei's age, an age that was not scientific at all. Texts like, "From the rising of the sun to the going down" suggested that the sun rose and went down when it was the earth that was going up and down and not the sun. But that does not change anything about the truth of scripture.

And never forget to number your days. The older think they have wasted their time, yet the young still think they have enough time at their disposal.

Who remembers the five foolish virgins that 'had all the time' in the world. They thought they could prepare anytime when the time was right.

'When the time is right, I will start that life-changing program. When the time is right, since I still have many days, I will....'

Days are too many until they are numbered.

A heart of wisdom dictates to you that time is always up. However, it reminds you that you have stayed on the mountain far too long, and it is time to make the next move.

6 REDEFINING THE FUTURE

The Creative Source

For let a man once have the idea that God has special plans for him, which he must further by his aid, and he will pluck up his heart and strain his understanding to get the better of all things and be their master. - **Thomas Mann**

One of the greatest questions I have had to ask myself was whether the future was rigid and foreordained or plastic and pliable. Was it made of clay such that I could mould it, or was it an impervious immovable rock? I asked myself whether it was a mountain standing solid out there or a fluid and pliable possibility. In other words, could I put my hand out there and create it for myself? Could I have a hand in the creation of that thing called the future, my future?

Was the morrow going to dawn without my aid or doing, or could I have a say in it? Could I determine the movements of my planets, or were they fixed like the milky way galaxy? Had I come into this world as a tourist to ogle, or was I brought here as a tiller of my garden like old Adam? Did I come here as a mover and a shaker or as a reed to be moved and shaken by any wind that blows by? Those were important questions in my life, and they should be yours too. Those are the questions the answering of which might determine what your life ultimately becomes.

The Yoruba language has a profound word, 'Iwaju', which means everything, 'future.' The time that is yet to come. It bears an absolute assurance that the future will undoubtedly unfold, whether beautiful or bitter. Tomorrow is guaranteed. As in, your tomorrows are guaranteed, and you are the guarantor.

The word also means that the future is not pre-determined. How beautiful is that? Imagine being told that you determine your future. That is a significant assertion. What this means is that your future is in your hands.

Therefore, the question becomes not, 'How strong are you or how prepared are you to face the future. Because if we talk about you facing the future, it means that the future is rigid, and you will face it like a tourist finds himself facing the Sphinx in Egypt or the Kilimanjaro in Tanzania.

The future can be attracted by the beauty within and the outlook you have about yourself. The energy inside of you has an appeal on its own.

As a Pastor, I have met young people radiant with this kind of energy. I could always predict what the outcomes of their lives would be, and I was never wrong. Like attracts like. Those who have that kind of energy have always done better than their opposites. The gloom and doom that often hovers the Earth you must avoid like a plague.

Let flowers bloom in your heart like springtime, for indeed, this is the spring of your life because you are alive. To be alive is an excellent opportunity to assert yourself. To declare yourself in any way is gratitude to God for bringing you down here.

I remember my school days, university days, to be precise. They were full of the energy of anticipation. Most students exuded that kind of energy. Yes, we lived in the present, but the greatest energy of those days was the energy of people who anticipated success and greatness in the morrows.

In our days, maybe because of segregation or poverty, if you made it to university, you were smart, you were special, you were amongst the future elite of black society, and that felt great, that landed a positivity in your life that is unimaginable. When you were back in the township, people respected you, and they respected your future. They knew that you were going to become somebody. The feeling of that society was also within you. You felt what they felt. Even though it was just a feeling, you have no idea what it did to us. This is a feeling world.

In my day, being at university was a guarantee that even if you did not make it that great in life, the minimum success would be that you would at least become a middle-class citizen. Even when you went back home during the holidays, people looked at you with that eye. You were already amongst the elite. That was the energy that circulated amidst us when we were at school. That was very positive energy. It rubbed onto you each day of your life, and it was a great rubbing too.

That energy must never abate in you. That is the energy of little children. That energy is the driver of all success. This is the energy of little children, which Jesus said, 'if you be not like little children, you will not enter the kingdom of God.' That energy is the gateway to the kingdom of God. When you see little children play around, there is no guilt or failure in their minds, only joy unspeakable and full of glory, and that is how we should live our lives.

There is no little child that is a failure, and it is not easy to take the bliss out of a little child. Failure in children is what we adults inculcate and teach into them. The happiness, the care-free-ness, the joy of life of the days of childhood, *Ake* in the Yoruba language, should be maintained throughout life. And that condition was supposed to be the permanent condition of mankind. Bliss! And I will tell you why?

God is not sadistic. He did not create you except for his delight and your own too. Therefore, in the good book, He says, "For I know the plans have for you," declares the LORD, "plans to prosper you and not to harm you, plans to give you hope and a future..."

THE EARTH IS THE LORD'S, AND ALL THE FULLNESS THEREOF

In the beginning, there was creation, God did it effortlessly in six days, and it would exist for eternity. By so doing, he set a tone for mankind and all the creation, that creation is the norm. Can I drive it in our often thick skulls that creation is the norm? We are first and foremost creators. Every single one of us.

In the art industries, music, theatre, literature, movies, they designate certain people as creatives, but all of mankind is creative. Not one breathing individual must be excluded from that designation. Unfortunately, most of us live in the negation of that reality because we are misaligned with the Higher Power. My children have my genes, and so does God's. Sometimes I sit down and watch my children go around, and I am amazed at how much of me they are. So does God, or so should He. We should give Him reason to.

A friend of mine met me in a hotel and almost did not recognise me because I had left my hair to grow and he said to me he thought I was my son. Think about it, he thought I looked like my son, which is funny because it is my son who looks like me.

"The future will undoubtedly unfold, whether beautiful or bitter."

Can you imagine that confusion between you and God? Somebody confusing you for God? Own image, own likeness!

We need to be in sync with ourselves and with the Higher Power to get to that place. When the 'Cosmos', which is originally a Greek word, meaning both "order" and "world," was created, it was to be an empire for humans, a complete sphere of *rulership*. For mankind, it was your domain where you would dominate, multiply in your gifts and subdue the Earth.

The world is so perfectly harmonious and impeccably put for your success and sustainability. God created the world and all its resources before he created man. That is very telling about the provisional element in God. So what happened? The order has maintained throughout the life of the Earth. The moon still shines and brightens the nights, and the galaxy of the stars in the milky-way still scintillate and glitter.

Sadly, only inanimate nature obeys God, and we are the only disobedient ones. Disobedient in our lack of faith. The Holy Book says that 'without faith, it is impossible to please God.' I dare to say that this faith hinted about in that statement is faith in God and faith in yourself and destiny.

Humans fell from grace, and we fell short of the glory as we tripped and started operating below our potential and mandate. In so doing, we lost the original place of our destiny in God. In this place, we would become co-creators with God and His greatest delight. He would say of us, like He said of Job in the book of Job, to the chief villain himself, Satan, "have you considered my servant Job?"

We need to find ourselves in that particular space. By so doing, we will find our desired future and embrace it.

We need to bounce back to our former glory and be the radiant children of God again. It is the purpose of this book to reinvent you, to assist you to get back to that path. In this world, many things will derail you, so you should always be focused.

The statement 'the spirit is willing, but the flesh is weak' is a profound statement. I have looked at the lottery lines and found people who were lowly and looked like they had no ambition in life, queuing there, and then I thought everybody wants to get ahead in life, even rich. It is the manifestation of the willing spirit, but the weakness of the flesh is that getting ahead could be achieved through the lottery.

Once in a while, somebody wins the lottery, but it is not something we should even consider since it is only one out of millions of people. And funny enough, most people who win the lottery lose all the money soon after because they suddenly have a lot of money they were never trained to handle.

There was a beautiful song back in the day by the Commodores entitled, "Easy come easy go." You are a gardener who earns R500 a week, and then you win ten million. What are you going to do? You think the money is infinite, and in two years, if even that long, it's all gone, and you are back to your R500, and you think that it is all witchcraft. Talking about witchcraft, I believe that it is your own personal craft. I think that people bewitch or *witchcraft* themselves. "As a man *thinketh* in his heart, so is he," really means that the greatest witch in your life could only be yourself.

You must understand that I am not saying that there is no witchcraft out there because there is. All I am saying is that even that kind of witchcraft, the door of that entering your life is in your own hands and that most of the mysticism in your life is done by your own self. I wish you can forgive me for being harsh, but that is the naked truth.

I wonder who was the originator of the phrase '*naked truth*', but I want to believe that he must have been a clothe-maker who saw what clothes made of men and women. He saw how we publicly lied about who we were when clothed in silk and cotton against how we looked when naked.

In an ancient Kingdom, a certain King wanted his daughter to marry a man that possessed eternal or future-proofed virtues. So he sent his men to go searching for people with a limitless measure of greatness. - Kingly men, in a manner of speaking. They searched the land with great diligence and asked folks everywhere in his kingdom if such men existed. They found several of those in different places and brought them to the presence of the King. Then, on an appointed day, the parade began.

Men of diverse talents and gifts were paraded before the King, potential suitors for the King's beautiful daughter. At the parade sat the King on his throne, his beautiful queen and his most *bedazzling* daughter, who was the subject of all the furore.

The parade began.

First, in the parade, a man with vast riches and wealth appeared, and the man seemed resourceful and competent enough to spoil the Princess. In the eyes of the King's men, here was the man that could make the Princess, *princessly*.

He had everything that could be required by one who was the daughter of a powerful monarch.

So the man tried to woe the King's daughter with material wealth, and to his dismay, he was dismissed out-rightly from the face of the King.

'That,' said the King, 'is not what I am looking for, for my daughter. I've got all that, and therefore she's got all that too.' In other words, you are bringing nothing to the table, as the English would say, coal to Newcastle and as South Africans would say, coal to Witbank, Emalahleni.

The second man was brought up, a strong man, well-built with biceps and triceps.

The King's warriors were thoroughly impressed, as they

couldn't match their physique to this great giant. They picked him because they thought that the Princess would love his physique since the myth went around that princesses loved the warrior types. The man walked in half-naked to show off his physique, and it was impressive to the eye.

The King was not impressed, and he began to engage this man in conversation to pick his mind. His Majesty wasn't impressed by what came out of his head. He found it empty of all that mattered and full of the peripheral everything else. So Muscle-man was dismissed too, to the disappointment of the King's men.

"Without faith, it is impossible to please God."

The King thought for a moment, muscle, power without brains would be disastrous to any kingdom. Physical prowess, in other words, brawn, does not build kingdoms. If you put muscle upfront, just the raw of it, the future will be futile, the King thought.

As you would guess, the fellow failed the test and ate humble pie to the surprise of the warriors that scouted him.

The wise King knew the recipe, the elements that he wanted out of his man. The King's monarchy was not patriarchal. The next ruler was going to be his daughter. The kingdom would be ruled by a queen when he died, and the man who married his daughter needed to be kingly.

The King waited for the next man on the parade. He was getting a little tired of his men's incompetence in recruiting the kind of guy he wanted. Then came a gentleman with an exceptional ability to read the signs of the times. A man of *cyclopedic* knowledge and erudition. He was glib of tongue and pleasing of speech.

The man was rumoured to belong to the descendants of *Issachar*, who were able to read the signs of the times. He had a rare quality about him and was artful in presenting himself before the King.

He showered the King with praises as he was entering the King's Courtyard. He ushered himself with great poesy like the courtiers of ancient Khemet. He rhymed his subtle thoughts, couching his speech in poetic and high sounding words.

He carried with him a deeper understanding of the Palace's workings and what the King would have wished for. At his illustrious entrance, everybody was *bedazzled,* and the King's façade melted in utter delight. Notwithstanding that the King took a liking to him, the Princess too was smitten.

Future secured! ▪

7 THE TEMPLE WITHIN

Exploring Your Divine Connection

Guard your heart with all diligence, for out of it are the issues of life. - **King Solomon**

Growing up, I have seen two sides of the human story — Happy humans and unhappy humans. And then I have also seen very happy humans and very unhappy humans, almost to the point of depression. But, unfortunately, I've seen a lot more of the unhappy side of the human story than the happy one.

We have heard this expression so many times, "It's hard to be a human." But, unfortunately, we have also seen this with our own eyes too many times.

To be born is simple; you are not involved in the process. The complexity comes when you have to live. Yet life is supposed to be exciting and straightforward, as you can observe with the little ones. Even nature itself, left untouched by the often harsh hand of man, demonstrates that the ease at which nature lavishes left to God or itself shows us that life was meant to be easy.

We are supposed to have wonderful souls in this often so broken world. But there are sceptics out there who preach that life is a struggle, that we are born to be doomed. So, do we join the sceptics, the critics and the *doomsayers* who see no beauty in being human, or do we continue being the radiant lights of the earth?

You must understand that the *doomsayers* are not necessarily out of context; they derive their story from the naked realities of their times. They are often just realists. People who see with their naked eyes and interpret the world as they see it.

The Holy Book says, "the just shall live by faith and that we walk not by sight but by faith." Or at least we should.

Often there is so much negativity out there, especially during times of crises like the world experienced in 2019, 2020, and 2021 with the Covid-19 pandemic or as experienced during economic depressions, beginning with the economic depression of the 1930s in the modern era. Although there were many before that, they might not have been called economic depressions. In our agrarian past, they were simply called years of famine.

Perhaps choosing the right perspective and attitude in such matters is the hard part of being human too. And the thing about it is that you decide which groove your life is going to slide on.

Are you going to let the mood or the general spirit of the day permeate you, or are you going to guard yourself or your heart? Are you going to go with the flow of panic, or will you hold on to the higher truths of life? Are you going to live from within or from *without*? Are you going to allow what is out there to drive your life, or are you going to go inside of yourself to find and define your essence?

These are profound decisions every one of us has to make. As the earth rotates around its axis at a dizzying speed, you too have to find the axis around which your life rotates, and I say unto you, it is better that it rotates from the temple within you.

Even during the Great Depression of the 1930s, some people were not depressed or became poor. I am talking about people who never queued on the bread lines. People who asked, 'what depression?'

Zig Ziglar said, "I hear there is an economic depression looming; I have decided that I will not participate in it." [Paraphrase] It is always your decision, even during times when the world is going through its most atrocious periods.

In the previous chapter, we have established that you are the designer of your destiny. Designing your destiny requires, first of all, that you fall in love with yourself again. I am saying again because I have observed little children, that the bliss they have so much in abundance is the first love. In the book of Revelations, the author rebukes a church for losing their first love. To win in this life is about love and appreciation of yourself. To love your neighbour as you love yourself starts with loving yourself.

Before you choose that path and undertake that life's journey as a creator of your destiny, learning to appreciate who you are, becomes the most important open secret. A secret that you are bigger, better and wiser than your physical body that houses and carries you. To love is one thing; to appreciate is another. You are an immortal, spiritual being just having a physical experience. You are made in a superior image that transcends the world we live in, and your body is merely the spacecraft that traverses you into your orbit. Your body is important, but it is not who you are. You are a divine child of The Invisible One, whatever name you ascribe to Him.

Your authentic self is indeed concealed from the world out there. It is tragic if that being is hidden even to yourself. To love yourself has nothing to do with what you see in the mirror because what you see in the mirror is not yourself. Therefore, the statement 'to love yourself' is more profound than what meets the eye.

"Life is real! Life is earnest! And the grave is not its goal."

Your soul is immortal, and what people see is merely a habitat, your abode. Yet, this knowledge is the superior lever that should propel your adventures into the future unknown. Mostly we face the world as our bodies. But, imagine a man or woman who faces the world as a spirit. Oh, what is it that they can achieve!

King Solomon said, 'As a man thinketh in his heart so is he.' Do our hearts have thoughts? Yes. The heart is the operating system for our souls. The entrance to the heart is through the mind, where the guarding of the heart is supposed to take place.

As a spirit or spiritual being, your *physical-ness*, even your physical experiences should never be able to *de-focus* you and cause you to abort your mission in life, and as the profound Pico de la Mirandola would put it, "which is to transform yourself into higher forms which are divine."

In the great poem,

A Psalm of Life,

 Henry Wadsworth Longfellow goes,

Tell me not, in mournful numbers,
Life is but an empty dream!
For the soul is dead that slumbers,
And things are not what they seem.

Life is real! Life is earnest!
And the grave is not its goal;
Dust thou art, to dust thou returnest,
Was not spoken of the soul.
Not enjoyment, and not sorrow,
Is our destined end or way;
But to act, that each to-morrow
Find us farther than today.

Art is long, and time is fleeting,
And our hearts, though stout and brave,
Still, like muffled drums, are beating
 Funeral marches to the grave.

In the world's broad field of battle,
In the bivouac of life,
Be not like dumb, driven cattle!
Be a hero in the strife!

Trust no Future, howe'er pleasant!
Let the dead Past bury its dead!
Act,— act in the living Present!
Heart within, and God o'erhead!

Lives of great men all remind us
We can make our lives sublime,
And, departing, leave behind us
Footprints on the sands of time;

Footprints, that perhaps another,
Sailing o'er life's solemn main,
A forlorn and shipwrecked brother,
Seeing, shall take heart again.

Let us, then, be up and doing,
With a heart for any fate;
Still achieving, still pursuing,
Learn to labour and to wait.

A HIGHER AND NOBLE LIVING

You have a higher life, a noble calling and your temple within to nurture and protect you. Yet, your sacredness is hidden, and your true treasure is invisible. Albeit, to succeed, one needs to re-calibrate his heart and align it with that higher life — the domain of your purpose. This will require that you have a heart of understanding as King Solomon admonishes us.

King David writes, expressing his heart's desire to the Lord, "Teach us to number our days that we may gain a heart of wisdom." To number your days is not just to maximize your potential but even the potential of each day of your life. In his poem, A Psalm of Life, as previously quoted, the poet Henry Wadsworth Longfellow writes,

Not enjoyment, and not sorrow,
Is our destined end or way;
But to act, that each to-morrow
Find us farther than today.

"Teach us to number our days," that is the highest prayer. Such prayers are the prayers of the wise. Therefore there are wise prayers and foolish prayers. Higher prayers and lower prayers. You remember that the now, this moment, is material or the material for the creation of your future, which can usher you to a place of immortality, in an earthly way of speaking.

If immortality ever accrues to man, it shall accrue to such as will learn to number their days. Each day plays a huge role in our lives, shaping our destiny. Our future is delayed when each moment is wasted. This is when we need the Master of the Universe to **'Give Us This Day'** so that we may be wiser in discerning the times. So in all our asking, we need to request the creator and the sustainer of life to, "Teach us to number our days, that we may gain a heart of wisdom."

There are people who have lived many years ago who still frame our worlds, who still influence our lives. That is what I am talking about. So you begin to design and create your future life NOW.

Every action you engage yourself in today becomes the building block to your destiny, so it matters what you do today as every day of your life matters. 'Teach us to number our days, Oh Lord,' that we may gain a heart of wisdom.' The Psalmist here is praying to God to help him not to disregard the importance of each day.

Sadly, if this virtue is not harnessed, we run the risk of lowering ourselves into an abyss – a series of dark episodes of *unfulfillment*. This nonchalance, this disregard for the gift of time, if not dealt with, can eventually be the dominant element that would by default become the collective substance of your life, and ultimately your destiny. It is through the gift of time, as in your days, that you become, or unfold.

Never give up on the person you are becoming. We are all human beings, so we have been made, are being made, and we are also evolving. Your life path becomes equally a growth path if you can be able to number your days.

Each and every blessed day, you are either evolving into a better version of yourself or devolving into something less.

Insist on a positive outcome.

8 EMERGING LIFE

Anyone Can Change

Change is the constant, the signal for rebirth, the egg of the phoenix. - **Christina Baldwin**

No matter how long you have walked on the wrong path, it is not late to turn back and walk towards the direction of peace and the path of purpose.

The word repent is the Greek *metanoia,* which means change your mind. Anybody who can change their mind can change their life at any moment in time. Do not be afraid to make radical changes in your life where and when necessary. Often you will realise that your life does not get better by chance. It gets better by change.

The great George Bernard Shaw says, "Progress is impossible without change, and those who cannot change their minds cannot change anything."

Around the nineteen nineties in our country, the cult of

change management became very popular in the corporate and government sectors. Change Management Consultants went around and coined it big, preaching the gospel of change. The country was evolving from a segregated apartheid state to an inclusive non-racial state.

Minds, black and white, were still set according to the patterns of the past and change and change management were the imperatives of those golden days.

We've all heard the sayings, "You can't teach an old dog new tricks." Or, "A leopard never changes its spots." Also, some have even gone as far as saying, "The wolf changes his coat but not his character."

Many people believe that we're not really all that changeable in terms of changing our fundamental' essence.' But here's the good news: they're wrong. Over the past three decades, rapid advances in brain science, personality psychology and many other fields have made the answer to this question of deep change much more nuanced and simple.

It turns out that we *can* change a great deal about our fundamental characters. Here is what you need to know if you're going through or planning a significant change. Studies of people recovering from brain injuries and stroke have long suggested that our brains are very adaptable, and we are capable of learning at any age.

Yes, picking up Mandarin might be harder at 70 than it would be at age seven, but you can learn a new language or skill at any age – just as stroke victims can relearn how to speak, using different parts of the brain. Not only does this brain plasticity make us more adaptable and flexible than we imagine, but it also extends to more profound aspects of our personality, such as levels of shyness or self-discipline.

BE GROUNDED IN YOUR PURPOSE

No life grows great unless it is thoroughly focused and disciplined. It has to be rooted in its fundamentals and in the true values of humanity, even divinity. You must have ground rules and live by them, strictly. You must know your purpose in life and pursue it vehemently without compromise.

They say that a postage stamp sticks to the letter until it arrives at its destination, so should you with your purpose. To be grounded is to stick.

"Anybody who can change their mind can change their life at any moment in time."

There will be many distractions, and one would need to steer the ship and stay grounded. Ships make great metaphors in this regard, especially the older types with sails that were driven by winds. The captain had a destination, yet the winds blew *whithersoever* they listed. So the captain had to steer the ship or boat to his desired destination, often against the will of the winds. Story of your life, isn't it?

Even then, something else was added to the science of navigation. They studied the winds, the easterlies, the westerlies, the southerlies, the northerlies, the typhoons and their seasons, and they learnt how to use them or co-operate with their movements to their advantage, and even how to fight them when there was a need to do so.

As every tree will tell you, being deeply rooted will hold you firm when the winds blow heavy. But, word of caution, 'never look too high if you haven't firmly rooted yourself.'

The four winds that blow from every side can be too tyrannical. Yet as I said, you can learn the game of the winds and defeat them. The basics are that you've got to be rooted to your own ground rules, your modus Vivendi, and grounded to your purpose, your chosen destiny, to be able to stand the storms of this life, especially if your aims are lofty.

FINDING MEANING AS YOU LIVE YOUR LIFE TO THE FULLEST.

There is a grievous rise of depression and dependency on *tranquilisers* in our days. When we try to reach out to this noble living and a life with a deeper meaning, there stands a world that demands more than we can offer. These unrealistic demands cause so many anxieties, and when humans cannot be in charge of their lives and destiny, fear and fatigue kick in. People then start looking out for '*something*' that would soothe their soul.

Many religions and so-called spiritual experiences have been birthed to try and satisfy that human craving. The other alternative is chemical dependency.

NEVER RELEGATE WHAT IS DEAR TO YOU.

There are so many things that demand our attention and sometimes impose their importance on our daily lives. These things need to be frequently evaluated. Your time is too valuable and critical to assign to unworthy causes. You also have limited time to spend in this life where you will not yield a good return.

Farmers plant their seeds in soils that will give them the greatest yields. Nothing else makes sense.

Of all sacred things, there are things that your life hinges upon. Your happiness being one of them requires that you jealously protect it. The good book elevates this fact when it says, "The joy of the Lord is our strength." Nothing should ever stand between you and your joy, which yields inner peace. Happy people have a strength that unhappy people cannot match. A happy you calibrates at a much higher level than his opposite.

DEEPEN YOUR ESSENCE

The soul is more alive than the body. It is what gives life to it (the body) and keeps it alive. It is the essential you. Your body is merely your tenantry in this bivouac of life. So, the soul also needs to be fed and nurtured even more than the body for it to be at its best. If it's alive, and it is, it can grow. That is why there are people in history who have been called Great Souls. Feed it, and you will see. As they say in *kasi* lingo, *faka imali u zo bona*, loosely translated *as* "invest in it, you will see the yield thereof.

Our soul is intricate and integrated with the Universe we live in. First, find a way to tune in with the music of the Universe. Next, you need to deepen that essence of yourself. This is done through prayer, fasting, meditation, scripture reading, and different other practices and rituals in different religions. For one to grow greater, be fulfilled and be perfect in imperfection, this is imperative.

If you are going to change the world, you are going to have to change yourself first, the essential you.

When your soul is deepened, then suddenly you begin to vibrate at a higher level than your human flesh, and you can tap into higher frequencies in spiritualism that will make the inhibitions of the earth not the greatest forces in your life. Most people have just become too earthy, too clayey because of the neglect of the soul. Jesus stood at the sepulchre of stinking and four days dead Lazarus, his dear friend and looked up and said, "Father, I know that you *heareth* me always." What confidence! What a great sense of connectedness! What a great prayer! What happened thereafter demonstrates what I am talking about here in living colour.

On the other side of the coin, life can be challenging. While we often find ourselves living in an unjust world, great souls have always known that they can transcend that. Transcendence at this level is a spiritual force. We do not need to return evil with evil, but rather rise about the grime that often inhabits the earth and would inhibit us.

Deepened souls throughout history have been able to handle that with aplomb. If you can defeat darkness and still hold your radar, all the days of your life will be light and bliss. If you are not afraid of darkness and delight in the light, you are living the life.

You will say like the psalmist, "The Lord is the strength of my life of whom shall I be afraid."

The deepening of the essential you should be as frequent as the nourishing and washing of your body. We stuff our bodies with victuals three times daily at least and hope that the soul will catch up even though we nourish it so infrequently. It is purely unscientific that the tree you *fertilise* less will outgrow the one you nurture the most. So maintain balance in these matters as is in all others. I also talked about washing as a part of deepening the soul.

The world we live in often taints us with what is foul and filthy about it: hatred, anger, bigotry, injustice, *unforgiveness* and the whole shebang. Often you have got to find a place of quietness to cleanse yourself of your encounters with these elements. Ask for forgiveness and forgive because your purity, when you live in a world polluted by the smokes and puffs of evil might not be guaranteed. And this can weigh up heavily on the soul and derail you from your path.

"The deepening of the essential you should be as frequent as the nourishing and washing of your body."

When you deepen your spiritual core with diligence, you will soon discover your divinity, and the driving force of your life, the engine, so to say, will begin to roar in your favour.

Looking beyond the now, project into the future and totally accept the past you suffered, as most people have. Follow your heart and be singular in what you want and believe in. Do not be double-minded, two-tongued and indecisive about your wishes. Learn to listen more to the chirping birds and release your heart to your happiness. Make sure you find a place under the sun or the shadow of a tree where you can be tranquil and connect with a Higher Power. Pursue peace and happiness and stay connected.

Life challenges us to develop and grow into full maturity through all the experiences we go through. So each day presents an opportunity to craft a personal yet practical approach to *de-clutter* our lives. This will require that we have a deep desire to grow and deepen our spirituality. This will assist you to develop and design a compelling life experience for yourself. We need to find a life of more freedom, more contentment. When you are content, you begin to approach life lighter and not burden yourself with too much. You start to live and travel lighter, where less is more, and life is richer.

CONTRIBUTE TO MAKING THIS WORLD A BETTER PLACE

A deepened self begins to see the world with different eyes. The physical world suddenly becomes more beautiful and serene. Man begins to stand epic as a creature made in the image of God in his eyes. Any man.

We need to start to see the beauty and the humanity in others. We need to *de-focus* on their otherness and see their "*us-ness.*" We cannot be helpful and kind to others when we do not see ourselves in them. I urge you to distinguish your mission and ensure that you give yourself to humanity and be part of the brigade that is bent on building a world beyond class and social standing.

This should not be executed in the condescending spirit as it has often been observed in some so-called charitable organisations. It should not be "I am great, and you are small, and therefore I am helping you." It should not be done from an 'I am better' space. It should not be done to be seen by others as a form of an exhibition. Of course, it is not always possible, but ideally, it should be done in a place where the left hand does not see what the right hand is doing.

Unfortunately, most of what is called charity today has so much PR behind it that you know it is not done in the spirit I am encouraging. As for you, be sold out in adding a smile to the broken-hearted. Heal the sick with your grace and encouragement.

Lift humanity up wherever you can. Declare good news, there is so much that is toxic around us, the world is yearning for healers, and by healers, I do not mean it in any *therapeutical* terms. Make a difference in people's lives every moment you can.

LIFE-CHANGING EXPERIENCES

Two existential questions that have been asked throughout history are permanence and change. The question has always been, "how can humans live a fulfilling life in an ever-changing world if everything that they hold close to them can easily be taken away?"

Fact, the material world is ever-changing, and to avoid decline, one needs to adapt to this reality. The best way to deal with this reality is to detach from materials or material realities. Therefore if things change, you should accept them, then move on and *re-strategise.*

By detaching our souls from the material world, we begin to enter a life-changing experience where our lives would find true meaning and value. When our minds perceive a different world, then 'our senses do' so too. Suddenly we become the new citizens of this new world and its realities, and we are born again.

We suddenly have the strengths and the mind to live again in the new environment. We are still the same winners who won yesterday and could still win today, albeit in a totally different environment.

And so, if there's ever anything that is constant and guaranteed in this life, it is '*change*.' Yet your mind needs to manage this change so that it doesn't overwhelm you, but you build your way into the new changed environment, little by little.

Our mortal beings are offered a certain period to be on earth, so we live for a relatively short time and disappear for eternity.

So what we do with our lives matters the most. Our time here is limited, and it would require that we don't only prioritise it but jealously protect it. We need the light that speaks pure direction into our lives and gives us insight into the future, today.

It was James Gordon, MD, who said, "It's not that some people have willpower and some don't. It's that some people are ready to change and others are not."

9 SELF-ORDAINED ROYALTY

Leading Like King David

Deliberation is the function of the many; action is the function of one. - **Charles de Gaulle (War Memoirs)**

In the entire Christian world, even Muslim, or even other religions, the name David, King David is well known and spoken about liquidly. The David and Goliath story has become a metaphor in all the world of literature. The question that history scholars often ask is, "Is King David mythology or history? Are we once again being given the story of Adam and Eve?" Because Adam and Eve are so pre-historic, there is no referencing the validity of their historicity.

Those who hang up to that story only do so by faith because there is no validating that any other way. I buy the story of Adam and Eve because I believe in the Holy Book, even though there are many stories of creation out there. One decides what one believes in, and I have decided that I believe in the 'Word of God.'

Whatever you believe in must work for you, and what I believe in does work for me. And that is enough for me. So whatever you believe in that works for you, keep believing it. I am not writing this book to try to convert you to my ways; if anything, I am trying to convert you to your own ways.

In the case of the story of King David, I dug into the annals of history and mythology, and while the story of David sounds fantastic, I have found out that it is not ahistorical. The Jews are amongst the few races extant in the world that have been very preservative of their history.

There are times called *pre-historical* times, and this story does not belong there. It might sound fantastic, but there are a lot other fantastic stories that happened in the present time than that. So, there was once a Philistia, and there was once an Israel in the history of time. There was once a David, and there was once a Goliath, and the two were involved in a duel, and the smaller man won. Having dispensed of that, let me take you to a time, a long time ago and through the events of those days.

It's a clear sky day in Bethlehem, and *ole* Jesse has summoned 'all' his sons to gather at the family pavilion, this time not to discuss livestock and real estate, the businesses the family was in. Okay, all his sons, according to what he thought was all, had gathered for the occasion.

The *Bethlehemite* has to prepare his sons, for one of them is about to be anointed and crowned a King by the Prophet Samuel.

It was, for the old man, a momentous occasion. Israel had had only one King, and one of his sons was going to be the next? He was excited but not necessarily surprised.

He was the great-grandson of Boaz and Ruth, remember them? According to the chroniclers, Boaz was the wealthy landowner and a great man of Israel, a true 'man of substance' who had employed young men and women to work in his estate. Ruth was a Moabite who found true happiness in her marriage to this great man, though it was short-lived, as her husband dies on the first night of their marriage. However, the marriage is blessed with a man-child Obed. This Obed would become David's grandfather — a lad who would later become King.

SO INTERESTING HOW EMPIRES BEGIN.

Jesse' sons are on the wait; hurriedly, the Prophet brings his horn along, abundant with oil, to anoint the next King of Israel. There is great anticipation, and every head is thirsty for the olive oil. Yet the King to be, has not even received an invitation to the parade.

Let me digress. You know there are so many of us, who never got the 'memo' to participate in events that would change our lives forever. Somewhat by divine impartation and direction, when the lot had fallen upon us to rule, we did not flounder — we ruled.

So the main man of this provocation did not get the memo or the invite. Personally, I prefer inviting myself because you can easily be neglected.

True greatness never happens by invitation; it is only the gate-crasher's lot. You have to invite yourself to the occasion. But this was a totally different situation because there was a divine element to it.

In this instance, the one that was not invited or thought about was saved by the seer and his integrity and faithfulness to the one who called and mandated him. The shepherd boy was overlooked by his father and brothers. Even though he had killed Goliath and given victory to Israel, they still thought there was nothing Kingly about him.

Maybe his age, his fragile beauty, his built, his *sweet-natured-ness*, his vocation or whatnot. The young man was, if anything else, not kingly. Do not trust the world to look at you, bet on the world to overlook you, but take a look at yourself, for that is the only look that matters.

"Many of us, never got the 'memo' to participate in events that would change our lives forever."

The David who killed Goliath had a good look at himself; he would not participate in his overlook. You should hear him affirm himself and his God at the occasion where he challenged the giant. It is never how the world looks at you; it is how you look at yourself.

'As a man *thinketh* in his heart, so is he,' said the wisest of all. Back to our initial tale as told in the Holy Book.

So David is away caring for his father's sheep, calves to be precise. A family responsibility he wouldn't delegate to anybody. He was a good shepherd, by the way. It is important that whatever you do, whether shepherd or floor sweeper, you do with great aplomb. Martin Luther King Jr said, "If a man is called to be a street sweeper, he should sweep streets even as Michelangelo painted, or Beethoven composed music or Shakespeare wrote poetry. He should sweep streets so well that all the hosts of heaven and earth will pause to say, 'Here lived a great street sweeper who did his job well.'"

David was such a great shepherd that he walked from that vocation to kingship. Every job you occupy is a stepladder — a stepladder to somewhere greater. Those who despise the day of small things are simply despising destiny. Small is the mother of great, little is the mother of large. Everything that you do is a door-opener to something greater.

Wherever you are in life, if you can look up, you can get to the next or higher place.

There is no greatness that would not be able to do what is regarded as a menial job except greatly. I think that David loved being a shepherd. It was the least important job in the family, but it was important that he put passion to even the last line of significance in the family network.

He found life and meaning in that menial job. Being a shepherd took him away from the world of man, as Thomas Hardy would put it, 'far from the madding crowd.'

The book of Psalms, of which he contributed a lot to, is not just music. It's also poetry, prophecy and inspiration.

Not too many kings could boast of so much talent while still being warriors of note.

That space, the shepherd space, is where he was able to create his music, to create his poetry, and to engender his closeness to Jehovah. One person in the whole Bible, who was able to create *closeness* to God without meeting him face to face like Moses and Jesus, was King David. Looking after the sheep and lambs was his lot, and it was there in the grazing fields that he infused His love for God and His covenant.

The quietude that is found in shepherding has created great leaders for Israel. Jacob, the patriarch, was once a shepherd, so was Moses the deliverer, and then David, the one who became the warrior King.

Perhaps I should throw a hint, that isolation, finding moments to be alone, drifting away from the noisome noise of the world we live in, is a very important thing for one to do.

We talk a lot about air pollution because we, of course, need air for our physical survival but we need to save ourselves from noise pollution too, because we need that for our spiritual survival.

Perhaps we all should find moments to be shepherds in our lifetimes. Moments to tend sheep, moments to be alone with nature. That is how you nurture your soul. That is how you get to hear the voice within.

When David penned down Psalm 23, "The Lord is my shepherd, I shall not want," he is now a matured man, yet those elementary and foundational virtues are now guarding his adult life. He had learned great lessons from daily shepherding. He is the Lord in this poem, the Lord of his sheep, and he parallels that to his relationship with his God. David was a student even as he was a shepherd. The Lord is my shepherd is also equivalent to the Lord is my teacher. He was being taught great lessons directly from the source of life Himself. That is why he became the person that he became.

It is possible to learn from God himself directly, but for that, you need to stay in a silent space. David was young and learnt his lessons early. Learning early is a great advantage. That is why the Bible says, 'teach a child in a way he should go, and when he grows older he will not depart from it.' This is how you avoid adult repair, learning early, sticking to the basic human values that you gathered growing up.

Let us go back to our original story again.

The Prophet Samuel had to call for a second parade, and by divination, a shepherd boy is destined to be in it: 'The prophet Samuel then said to ole Jesse, "Are all your sons here?" Jesse replied in second thought and said, "There remains yet the youngest, but behold, he is keeping the sheep." In a manner of speaking, it is like he is unimportant; that is why when you asked for my sons, I did not include him.

David was overlooked from day one, so are most people who ultimately become great. The teacher who named Rolihlahla Mandela, Nelson, which was not his name, probably did so because he did not take him seriously. You don't just give people names like that without even getting the approval of their parents unless you think they don't matter.

Samuel said to Jesse, "Send and get him, for we will not sit down till he comes here." And he sent and brought him in. Now he was ruddy and had beautiful eyes and was handsome. And the Lord said to Samuel, "Arise, anoint him, for this is he."

Then Samuel took the horn of oil and anointed him in the midst of his brothers. And the Spirit of the Lord rushed upon David from that day forward.' (I Samuel 16:11-13)

As Ezra, the High Priest, would declare, 'Arise for this matter is your responsibility, we will support you, so take courage and do it.' Here, Ezra is admonishing the King of Persia to commission a Leader from the Jewish Community to carry out a mission' a noblest of missions to return to Zion, thereby establishing the Temple and the Kingdom. When Ezra returned from Babylonian exile, he himself orchestrated the return of the Torah. And so, like Ezra, David was mindful of his mission and what needed to be done. Empires are built by those who dare to ARISE.

BUILDING ZION – THE CITY OF DAVID

Have you ever thought of having a City with your name on it, well, not necessarily brick and mortar—a city of your calling and purpose? I am still endeared to the whole idea of empire building, but perhaps we should go physical and structural; that is when we think and talk about building things like cities. Zion, which still exists today, is called the city of David.

Like everything else, cities are man-made; they are not like mountains and valleys which we found here or nature forms as nature should. If you have ever seen the skyline of cities like Manhattan in New York or the beautiful sky-touching structures in Dubai, you will develop an appetite for city building.

In a metaphorical sense of speaking, I think you should develop a thinking in that direction.

You should think about this and perhaps build your own city. Nothing stops you from that. Earlier on, I spoke about a man called Oral Roberts who created a city within a city called South Tulsa, in Tulsa, Oklahoma, with an offering or collection of $26. A man who, when he saw the collection, he did not despise its *measliness,* and he proclaimed that 'with this ($26), I will build a university.' This university became much more than that. It became the City of Faith, the Prayer Tower, a suburb and a whole lot more.

David returns to Jerusalem, having driven the Jebusites out through a convincing conquest. He renames the City Zion, and it's gracefully called the 'City of David' — the beginning of an Empire with no end. To this day, Mount Zion is the place where Yahweh, the God of Israel, dwells, the place where He is King (Isaiah 24:23) and where he has installed His King, David (Psalm 2:6.) according to the Holy Book. This is the King that was once a shepherd boy.

David enters life as a humble shepherd. He rises to establish a dynamic dynasty and becomes a central figure in geo-political space that would later shape a great nation as we now know it. Israel.

The history of it is that King Saul's Army is ridiculed by circumstance. He fails to reach a decisive victory against an enemy tribe, the Philistines. This is not because of any inadequacies in him, but the fact that he disconnected himself from the Higher Power that initiated him into his position.

Along comes David, armed with only a sling. He picks up five stones from a riverbed, and together with a sling, they combine to create a stealthful and fearsome weapon. But not only is he armed with the physical weaponry, but he is also armed with faith in the Higher Power, the Lord who is his shepherd.

A giant named Goliath, carrying a huge bronze spear and a seemingly impenetrable shield, he confronts. This is Israel's nemesis. The Israelites were frozen in fear, even so, was their King—the only one who is outside of that emotion is young David.

He challenges the giant, he dares him, and he says I can take him on. He talks down to him. He even goes genital, calling him uncircumcised.

"Empires are built by those who dare to ARISE."

Yet, such a kind and brave act would later breed enmity between him and King Saul. Even though David later married Saul's daughter, Michal, and became a close friend of Saul's son Jonathan, an intense rivalry developed between the young new general and the King, even though the rivalry was one-sided.

Saul even began to plot to kill him. David had little choice but to flee to enemy territory, until the day Saul is rejected by God, and that's when the Empire Builder, KING D!, entered the scene.

David's first day of executing his royal duties was not of less drama than his first day at war. He chooses a unique assignment, that of connecting his earthly kingdom, the Judean kingdom, with that of a Higher Power. He brings back the Ark of the Covenant, the legendary artefact built some 3,000 years ago by the Israelites to house the stone tablets on which the Ten Commandments were written. This is more than just symbolic to King David; it is the embodiment of the life and blood of a nation that has a chance to build its empire. So this heirloom authenticates the story about Moses and their faith in a God. And David dares anyone who chooses to undermine that.

In fact, the story of the Ark of Covenant, is well documented in 2 Samuel 6:1-7 and 1 Chronicles 13:9-12. The ark is being transported, the oxen that are pulling the cart stumble, and here is a man by the name of Uzzah looking and chooses to assist God.

He takes hold of the ark.

God's anger burns against Uzzah, and He strikes him down, and he dies. According to the Law of Moses, touching the ark was in direct violation of God and was to result in death.

This was a means of preserving a sense of God's holiness and the fear of drawing near to Him without appropriate preparation.

So David values the importance of surrounding his Empire with Deity, and what a better symbol than the Ark of the Covenant?

He confidently unites all the smaller kingdoms and tribes of Israel under a single powerful monarch. Eventually, all of the regions in Canaan came under David's control. David then expanded his territory until Israel had become the dominant state in the Levant, absorbing the nations of Ammon, Moab, and Edom. David didn't just emerge as a successful and an ideal king, as successful in peace as in war; he was truly a beloved in God's eye as well as in the eyes of the people.

God, the Captain of the host, would eventually say about him, "I have found that David, son of Jesse, is a man after my own heart, who will do all my will."

PERSONAL INADEQUACIES

David was a good human being, but like everybody else, he also had his weaknesses. There was fallibility that almost dominated his entire personal and political life. His reign was filled with conflict and tragedy. Many times King David would compromise his reputation.

One notable act was his pursuit of the beautiful Bathsheba, who was already married to Uriah, one of his top commanders.

David ordered him to be placed in the front ranks of a planned assault against the Ammonites, where he was duly killed. So David, the beloved of God, was no perfect man. This is very important to note.

Abraham, the second man (Noah having been the first) in the story of God after the fall of Adam, was not a perfect man either. He was a bigamist, amongst other things, but he was still a friend of God. He was given the stamp of righteousness not because of his perfection but because of his faith in God.

This much lauded King David sets a trap for Uriah, hoping for him to be killed in the war, and it happens as planned. Who knows, Uriah could still have been assassinated by one of David's warriors while in battle because Uriah had fought battles and not died by the enemy's sword. Whatever occasioned, whatever the suspicions that I am trying to infuse into the old age story, Uriah dies.

So King David kills a man so he could marry his wife, and he still has a good piece of real estate in the Holy Book. We have all been kind to the King, but perhaps we have to be kind to ourselves, despite some of the things we often do wrongly. We should forgive ourselves before we even forgive King David.

Bathsheba enters into a mourning period for her departed husband, and David comforts her with tenderness. He ultimately worms his way to her grieving heart and marries her. She then conceives a child by the King.

Then she bears him a son. But the Prophet Nathan sternly rebuked David for his evil scheming because it had "displeased the Lord," and indeed, the baby died (II Samuel 11:27). David then repented before God, and in return, was promised that Bathsheba would bear him a second son. His name was Solomon.

As David grew older and feeble, Bathsheba extracted David's promise that their son Solomon would succeed him. And so it came to pass. His son Solomon is groomed to expand the empire that David is presiding over.

Here is a fulfilment of a promise as God has declare to David that "When thy days are fulfilled, and thou shalt sleep with thy fathers, I will set up thy seed after thee, that shall proceed out of thy bowels, and I will establish his kingdom. He shall build a house for my name, and I will establish the throne of his kingdom forever."

LONG LIVE THE KING!

The longevity of kingdoms rests on how they stay relevant. The continuous demonstration of their ingenuity and the maintenance of their originality even as they evolve is key. David's empire was divine, and its sustainability depended on superior powers.

"I will be his father, and he shall be my son: if he commits iniquity, I will chasten him with the rod of men, and with the stripes of the children of men: but my loving kindness shall not depart from him, as I took it from Saul, whom I put away before thee. And thy house and thy kingdom shall be made sure forever before thee: thy throne shall be established forever.'"

God had sworn by His name on David, which made King David unstoppable to the envy of his rivals.

And of His Kingdom, there will be no end

The lineage of David's Kingdom was perpetual up to the birth of the Messiah and beyond. This is why Matthew chooses to give us the genealogy of the Messiah to reflect the kingship of David and that of the Saviour.

"And the Lord God will give to him the throne of his father David, and he will reign over the house of Jacob forever, and of his kingdom, there will be no end."

The promise of the renewed life where the gentiles would bring wealth was what kept the treasury of David to being the most potent any man has ever produced. His wealth of writings would express a grateful heart and, at other moments, a regretful soul.

In all these, David feared no mere mortals but knew GOD was fighting all his battles.

10 AVOIDING DECLINE
Surviving the Future

The superior man, when resting in safety, does not forget that danger may come. When in a state of security, he does not forget the possibility of ruin. When all is orderly, he does not forget that disorder may come. Thus his person is not endangered, and his States and all their clans are preserved. - **Confucius**

Often when I go home to *Lekazi* or Soweto, where I grew up, I am confronted with the melancholic ruins of businesses of men who used to make it big in the *kasi* economy. Rich people we used to look up to. Some have been wiped out of the face of the earth. Others still have dilapidated buildings now rented out by people from sea-faring countries. Their children, who grew up like princes and princesses, not even being half a shade of what their parents were. In the worst cases, inhabitants of the streets and drink-holes.

I ask myself, what happened? Many theories abound in

ekasi. Some blame it on crime, some on the new dispensation, while others go blatant and blame it on witchcraft, hubris, even *utokoloshe* (mystic evil spirit).

I don't blame anyone for their theories, for they are all right. Instead, I blame myself for not having the answers.

It is this lack of answers that took me on a trip from the very present extremes and to the distant past to try to fathom this phenomenon of decline. I might be a little exacting in my illustrations, but I want you to be patient with me. I will narrate historically true stories, allegories and fiction to take you through this most intriguing of subjects; decline and how to avoid it and if it is even possible to do so.

In his illustrious work on "How The Mighty Fall", and why some companies never give in, Jim Collins raises a *utopian* and illusionary posture that individuals and companies take when they are up there — an assumption that they will never fail and that they are 'born for success.'

This illusion, which he calls 'hubris', becomes a state when arrogance creeps in and we dunce-like think that we are insulated from failure. It is when we get to that space that we falter. All extinct entities found themselves landing on that space and often could not figure out 'the hows' and wherefores of it. They had failed to constantly self-examine while still at the pinnacle of their hill.

Self-examination is always necessary for those who want to stay and remain successful. Decline creeps in like a thief by night. It is never barefaced. It's a creeper, and only a watcher can spot it.

Complacency is the downfall of organisations and individuals. Sitting down and relaxing in what you call achievement is dangerous because the world is fluid and marching on. Complacency — that is when the decline begins. In a simple way of speaking that is easily understood, that is when pride comes before a fall.

Of the empires that we remember, especially political, which one still remains?

Even in our personal lives, one needs to avoid and detect decline and place oneself on a trajectory that will bring keen alertness, *clear-headedness* and clarity of personal vision.

In other words, we should always know that to be and stand in the same place is dangerous and that what does not grow will ultimately rot or decline.

That is a fact of nature, and we can never soar above the realities of that. We must be like gardeners, watching our crops daily and tending them, fixing whatever seems to need attention, fumigating enemy insect predators away daily.

How are the mighty fallen

One of King David's most quoted statements outside of the Psalms is, "How are the mighty fallen in the midst of the battle! O Jonathan, thou wast slain in thine high places."

The Mayans Civilization

The Mayan civilisation has been heralded in ancient history as one of the foremost in human development. 'Most archaeological explanations for their collapse involve agriculture. The world economy was then predominantly agrarian. I think that agriculture is still dominant today. Like all large civilisations of the time, the

Mayans were heavily dependent on crops for their economic might — and of course, to sustain their vast workforce. The simplest explanation for the Mayans fall is that year-upon-year of low crop yield, brought on by the droughts, might have gradually diminished their political dominance and influence, eventually leading to full-on societal disintegration.

It's so unfathomable that a great Nation, such as the Mayans, could be brought down.

But even advocates of the drought hypothesis admit that the drought picture is not telling us the full story. "We know that there was already increased warfare and socio-political instability throughout the Maya area before the 9th Century droughts," writes Julie Hoggarth at Baylor University in Waco, Texas, who is a climate analyst.

Inter-city conflict is a pretty good way to break up a civilisation, too; it's possible that the Mayans just fought themselves apart. But that still leaves the question of the droughts and those well-fitting dates. Perhaps, then, it was a mixture of the two. As food stocks shrank during the dry decades, competition for resources would probably have become even more intense, perhaps eventually reaching a tipping point that caused the ancient Mayan civilisation to fracture irreparably.

Not that they did not try to mitigate against the dry season because, while the Mayans were famously great craftsmen, they were also environmental sculptors.

To grow enough food to feed their millions, the Mayans dug massive systems of canals, sometimes hundreds of miles across, which allowed them to drain and elevate the infertile wetlands which cover much of the Maya heartland, producing new arable land (some archaeologists call these "floating gardens"). However, the Mayans also cleared huge tracts of forest, both for agriculture and to make room for their cities. The deforestation to clear land for agriculture might have exacerbated localised drying effects, leading to more significant agricultural losses during drought.

Some scholars think that the Mayans skilled manipulation of their environment could have had a hand in their eventual collapse by somehow worsening the impacts of natural climate change.

"To be human is to be powerful, but it is also vulnerable."

A more indirect consequence of their agricultural prowess might simply have been that it allowed the population to grow too large, which might have increased their vulnerability to an extended food shortage and reduced their resistance to a drier climate.

Why am I bringing into this treatise the story of the Mayans? I am trying to demonstrate the need for foresight—the need for constant reinforcements in life and business.

There is one thing that you can appreciate about the Chinese's forward-looking thinking. There was a time when their leadership preached and forced upon their nation to grow their numbers so that they could later be able to dominate the world with just their sheer numbers. Then there was a time when they thought that their numbers were a disadvantage because suddenly feeding those numbers was a problem.

Forward-looking is very important. Leaders should be able to look into the future with a crystal glass, or they should rather retire.

I am writing this book from Africa, and I personally think that the main problem of this continent is leaders who are always looking into the past and obsessed with the present, their own pockets and have no eye for tomorrow.

Even the great Nelson Mandela did not think beyond the present. His reconciliation project of creating social cohesion was too short-sighted. As a country, we still have the very same problems that we had under apartheid. If I have to rate him, where future-thinking was concerned, he does not score any remarkable marks.

By the way, I know that it is not very popular to criticise that great Nelson, but I am writing this book for your enlightenment, and I want you to think. I am also not afraid of controversy. I am also not afraid to disagree with anybody who has an opinion in the world. So if you disagree with me, it's fine, do so but read on.

To me, it is such a joy to read a book that controverts my thoughts, that way, I grow.

I remember our early days as Christians, the church was so intolerant of different ideas that our preachers were almost like baked in the same bakery. You never heard anything different. This is inherently wrong.

The reason the Jews killed Jesus Christ was that he dared to speak against convention. He dared say that Moses was wrong, only right during his times, that the time for a Mosaic doctrine was over. So you go into the libraries of the world, and people want to tell you what you want to hear.

My head is not locked onto your chest; we are not Siamese twins, so there is no need for you to try to agree with me on all matters or on Nelson Mandela or anybody else for that matter.

There are two ways to sure decline; standing at the same place and not moving consistently and constantly.

The Holy Roman Empire

The English historian and parliamentarian Edward Gibbon penned the book Tour de Force. If I might say, "The Decline and Fall of the Roman Empire." He was greatly criticised for the volumes of his book, but mostly because his objectivity attacked the Christian, the Muslim and the other peripheral religions of his days. Of course, when you attack religious beliefs, you are going to be up for a serious counter-attack.

I am not necessarily vouching for him, but he nailed the facts, and he was unafraid to state in a book that a decline did take place of the so-called great Holy Roman Empire *nogal*, and I must applaud him for that.

The Roman Empire is not an empire that I applaud because it gave rise to imperialism and, ultimately, colonialism. There are those who want to assuage their consciences and say that colonialism benefited the Third World people. I simply forgive them for their dire lack of insight. They should ask us and not just engage in presumptuous conclusions about other people.

Be that as it may, we must necessarily accept that declinations happen in life and in the world at large. But as it is in the spirit of this volume, declines can be avoided. It would be great in all organisations if there were people employed to watch if they were progressing or declining.

It would be great if statisticians and visionaries would be engaged, whose sole responsibility would be to watch corporate progress or retrogression, external trends and best-practice. Sentinels who would forever be watching for the barbarians and their arrival and intended invasions.

Your life is not different from the story that I have just painted right now. My story about the Holy Roman Empire should not derail you from the fact that I am talking to you. I am not talking about or to empires. I am talking about and to you, the empire builder of today.

This book is only written to you in person. Everything I say to you might be in parables, anecdotes and allegories, but it is directed at you. Every story I throw in, I do so that you can understand your own personal situation.

If some corporates and nations with greater strategies and a strong balance sheet never survived decline, we've got to take a leaf out of that and act in a responsible manner. Decline is rot, and it exists in nature. How does rot happen? Anything rots if it's left unprotected or unpreserved. As easily as potatoes and tomatoes rot when unpreserved, everything else does so.

Dreams, visions, ideas and all the subliminal others that create futures are not immune from that. That is why procrastination is called 'the thief of time.' Procrastination is postponing that which you should do today to a day in the calendar called tomorrow, a day that does not exist.

Think about the story of the Holy Roman Empire, about the story of The Lehman Brothers, about Enron. Enron shareholders filed a $40 billion lawsuit after the company's stock price, which achieved a high of US$90.75 per share in mid-2000 had plummeted to less than $1 by the end of November 2001 through corruption (rot), lies, deceit and neglect. It was one of the biggest scandals of the century.

Galatians 6:7, in a candid yet threatening tone, reads, "Be not deceived; God is not mocked: for whatsoever a man soweth, that shall he also reap. There are two beings you can't mock or cheat. Your God and yourself.

"Decline can be avoided, detected and be reversed."

The kingpins of Enron were able to hide billions of dollars in debt from failed and corrupt deals and projects. In addition, the Chief Financial Officer, Andrew Fastow, and other executives misled Enron's board of directors and audit committee on high-risk accounting practices and pressured Arthur Andersen to ignore the issues.

That was the rot and decline of the century, but what other rots are taking place at personal levels? We all exclaimed at Enron with disdain, but most of us failed to look at ourselves inside or at our much smaller corporations. Remember the law of life dictates; 'as in the microcosm, so in the macrocosm.' What happened at Enron happens every day in our lives, but as I said earlier, it can be avoided. It was Jim Collins who said, "Decline can be avoided, detected and be reversed."

The U.S. Securities and Exchange Commission(SEC) began an investigation, and rival Houston competitor Dynegy offered to purchase the company at a meagre price. It was a good time for sharks to sharpen their teeth and for vultures to fly low.

in December 2, 2001, the deal failed, and Enron filed for bankruptcy under Chapter 11 of the United States Bankruptcy Code. Enron's $63.4 billion in assets made it the largest corporate bankruptcy in U.S. history until the WorldCom scandal the following year, in what you could call a diving competition.

Many executives at Enron were indicted for various charges, and some were later sentenced to prison. Arthur Andersen was found guilty of illegally destroying documents relevant to the SEC investigation, which voided its license to audit public companies and effectively closed the firm. By the time the ruling was overturned at the U.S. Supreme Court, Arthur Andersen had lost the majority of its customers and had ceased operating.

Enron employees and shareholders received limited returns in lawsuits, despite losing billions in pensions and stock prices. The executives were all charged with felonies after the allegations.

The moral of the story is that rot sets in, and then decline happens. It happens at the higher levels, and it also occurs at the lower levels, but the greatest of all things that I have mentioned is that it can be avoided at all levels.

THE STORY OF ATLANTIS

The story of Atlantis is a much-told story throughout history, even though it is ahistorical. Even as I write, the written account of the world is scarcely 7000 years old. So nobody would have been able to write about something that happened 9000 years ago, especially during Plato's era (427 BC – 348 BC) that would have been anything but fiction. Nevertheless, it is an allegory, and it tells my story perfectly — that even in an era of the greatest splendour and prosperity, decline can occur.

Plato's Greek mythology of Atlantis is a metaphor that will help us reach a perfect understanding of where this concept we are wrestling with is concerned. Atlantis is a fictional island mentioned in an allegory on the hubris of nations in Plato's works Timaeus and Critias, where it represents the antagonist naval power that besieges Ancient Athens, the pseudo-historic embodiment of Plato's ideal state in "The Republic."

Aristotle believed that Plato, his teacher created this story to teach philosophy. He used this story to help explain his ideas about governance and philosophy.

Plato creates a great fictional nation inhabited by beings that were half god and half human. These people created an enviable utopian civilisation and became a great naval power. Their home was made up of concentric islands separated by wide moats and linked by canals that penetrated to the centre.

The lush islands contained gold, silver, and other precious

metals and supported an abundance of rare, exotic wildlife. The greatness, prosperity and triumph of this fictional island-nation have occupied many hearts, and it has been passed down by generations of poets, novelists, priests, and others. The story concludes with Atlantis falling out of favour with the deities (gods) and submerging into the Atlantic Ocean.

So what happened?

How could such great peoples be annihilated to the point of non-existence? If this great and mystical Atlantis could be wiped into extinction, Plato teaches, what cannot be protected, is destroyed.

It is very important that you create, but also just as important is that you protect and preserve your creation and sustain it. Unfortunately, decline is a law of nature. What is neglected will naturally rot. This is true to business, relationships, real estate, assets and anything else that belongs to the earth. There is nothing on earth that can survive neglect.

Just like growth, rot happens little by little, and therefore it takes a keen eye to observe it. If you go into this life with the little by little mentality, you should be able to observe the negative little by little while making sure that the positive little by little dominates the course of your life.

I'm a lover of modern history, though economics dominates a larger part of my days and is a great occupier of my time when I'm in my study lounge. However, one of the ancient manuscripts that fascinates me to this day is that of Gibbon: 'How the mighty have fallen' is very important to me or the spirit of this text. To be on top is ecstatic; to suddenly be on the bottom is tragic. It is also very telling. It only means that somewhere down the line, there was a place or moment when neglect crept in.

According to Gibbon, the Roman Empire "succumbed to barbarian invasions, in large part due to the gradual loss of civic virtue among its citizens."

The parallels in our living years are so glaring. We have seen great, and mighty nations and corporations fall flat on their enormous bellies.

In a short script, we have all seen the mighty fall and exclaimed and asked like King David, "how have the mighty fallen." It is the 'how' that must be the case study for us to avoid such calamities in our lives and practices. And they can indeed be avoided. These phenomena are mostly incurable, but they can be avoided. As the adage says, 'prevention is better than cure.'

"To be on top is ecstatic; to suddenly be on the bottom is tragic."

When Rome was severely under attack, Gibbon coined a metaphor, 'the barbarians are at the gate', and that was his painful observation of a siege and a probable invasion. This was the beginning of the fall of Rome. That was an attack from without. It would be naïve to deny that decline often happens through outside forces, but that is secondary.

Before that even happened, Gibbon talks about the decline in civic virtues. This was the actual beginning of the fettering, an attack from within.

Arnold Toynbee, British economic historian and author of, amongst others, "Surviving the Future, once said, "Civilisations die from suicide, not by murder."

This can be juxtaposed in personal life with the inability to harness highly effective habits that are important for success in the individual's life and his practice. These inputs or lack thereof would eventually determine the output and the outcome. Where there are no sacrifices, individuals or enterprises never thrive.

"In Too Big to Fail: The Inside Story of How Wall Street and Washington Fought to Save the Financial System—and Themselves," Andrew Ross Sorkin chronicles not just an attempt to save the Financial Systems but also reveals the systematic decline of civic virtues by the big corporate leaders. He explains and argues this phenomenon so vividly, leaving nothing to the imagination. Then he inches in on the drama surrounding the bankruptcy of Lehman Brothers on September 15, 2008. Oh, what drama!

After several attempts to salvage itself, all discussions failed, and 'Lehman filed a Chapter 11 petition that remains the largest bankruptcy filing in U.S. history, involving more than US$600 billion in assets.'

As the Wall Street records would reveal later, 'the bankruptcy triggered a 4.5% one-day drop in the Dow Jones Industrial Average, then the largest decline since the September 11, 2001 attacks.'

To this day, this has been a Business School lecture on how

governments continue to fail to regulate big corporations and thereby failing to manage crises. Money market mutual funds, a key source of credit, saw mass withdrawal demands to avoid losses, and the interbank lending market tightened, threatening banks with imminent failure. The government and the Federal Reserve system responded with several emergency measures to contain the panic.

Robert Kiyosaki, who I religiously follow when it comes to financial literacy and investing, once predicted in his book 'Rich Dad Prophecy', this meltdown, adding that 'there's little investors can do but buy gold or silver and hope the Federal Reserve slows the slide.'

The slide, however, hasn't stopped and now ordinary people all over the world are catching a cold – Wall Street has sneezed.

Dealing with your Dark Age

Three thousand six hundred years ago, factors such as massive climate change, fires, and drought brought about the Mycenaean civilisation's decline. This dragged and launched the great Greece into a so-called 'Dark Age.'

The gods couldn't save the Greeks, or perhaps humans chose to be self-reliant and chose to replace deity with themselves in their development, to their demise. How many a time has a people chosen to play God only to bring misery to themselves?

Some things are superior to our souls, and that you find when you have to look *up* for solutions. At least it is important to sometimes look up to something or Somebody bigger than ourselves.

Since then, the Greek civilisation resumed in the 800s B.C. to become what it is today, Western Civilization.

The Bronze Age was to be the start of human advancement, and the Greeks bequeathed hope and courage to humanity. As they would say, 'rising like a Phoenix from 'ashes of despair into the buoyancy of hope.'

The Greeks never stopped innovating, never stopped building, and for many years they would avoid the decline of their civilisation.

If we have to be true to history, it must be mentioned that the Grecians were the students of the people of Khemet, ancient black Africa, now called Egypt.

We must never fall under the false illusion that the Greek civilisation was the first ever. So while I laud and mention the Grecians, I need to highlight that their most lauded culture and society was secondary.

As humans, our constant search for this higher life gives meaning to our pursuits. This makes us human, to believe that tomorrow can be better than yesterday. To be human is to be powerful, but it is also vulnerable, therefore constantly needing some Higher Power to insulate us and rescue us from annihilation that is forever courting us.

The Greeks relied largely on their gods for their survival. The founding fathers of this civilisation believed in the ideals of the gods' divine intervention and that of human development. They held true to the virtues of natural progression and that of ideal societies. They frowned upon the gradual corruption of human society. Where there is no moral duty to pursue, sooner or later, corruption sets in. When corruption sets in, it is the beginning of a decline.

Our spirituality is often being eroded by the demands put upon us by the material world. If we are not alert, such demands can often weigh our souls down. As in the Greek setting, the gods can never be happy when we are silent and not calling upon them and over-relying on ourselves. Self-reliance is a good thing, but over self-reliance is very limiting.

THE CASE OF THE MAPUNGUBWE KINGDOM

Located in the very north of South Africa, just below the Limpopo River, there lies some ancient ruins of the Mapungubwe Kingdom. In its quest for the mastery of the use of iron, the Kingdom grew in leaps and bounds between the 11th and 13th centuries.

> # "Our spirituality is often being eroded by the demands put upon us by the material world."

This Kingdom also prospered due to the sustainability of the savannah for cattle herding and its access to copper and ivory. These permitted long-distance trade and brought gold and other exotic goods to the ruling elite and the traders.

The Kingdom was sufficiently capitalised with a formidable centralised authority, which monopolised trade, wealth, production and distribution and could command labour to build large stone structures.

African cohorts formed the Kingdom of Mapungubwe with a deep sense of spirituality. It is this sort of religious association between the kings and rainmakers that was a vital necessity for agriculture in such a dry landscape. Spiritual rituals would, from time to time, be rendered to a Higher Power.

The king and his court dwelt in a stone enclosure composed of stone walls and had fortified houses built on the highest levels of the community's territory, a natural sandstone hill. The royal wives lived in separate dwellings from that of the king, purposely demarcated by several detached homes made from grindstones.

The kings were buried along with their predecessors at the top of the hill-site in a demarcated area away from the dwellings, while commoners were buried at the surrounding valley level. A wooden staircase connected the two levels, the sockets for the steps clearly visible in the sandstone cliff face.

Some grander residences dotted around the outskirts of the lower level town, which probably belonged to the king's male relatives. It is known that in Bantu society, such males, serious competitors for the king's position, were not permitted to live directly within the community.

TRACES OF TRADING

The Mapungubwe Kingdom is known to have been trading with other nations as far afield as India and China. Many carnivorous animal remains, and ivory splinters suggest that animal hides and elephant tusks were accumulated, probably for trade with coastal areas reached via the Limpopo River. The presence of glass beads, almost certainly from India, and fragments of Chinese celadon vessels indicate there was undoubtedly trade of some sort with other states on the coast, which in turn, traded with merchants travelling from India and Arabia by sea.

Contemporary with the Kingdom of Zimbabwe (12-15th century BCE), located to the north on the savannah plateau on the other side of the Limpopo River, Mapungubwe would also have benefitted from locally-sourced copper and the gold trade that passed through from south-west Zimbabwe to the coastal city of Kosala. Indeed, initially, Great Zimbabwe may have been a client state of Mapungubwe. However, the prosperity that trade links brought would likely have led to a strengthening of political authority in order to control and even monopolise.

But I am talking to you here about kingdoms that were. I am taking you through ruins. They make great museum pieces. But I say that there is no reason why they shouldn't still be here. The civilisations and their populations have been outlived by their walled ruins. The stones remain, while the people and their societies have vanished.

The stones remain because they did not transgress. Were they ruined, perhaps because they did know that "the axe is laid at the root of the tree?" That everything that lives and does not constantly examine itself is a prospect for decline? Was decline inevitable in any way? If it wasn't avoidable, I would not waste my time writing this chapter.

The Kingdom of Mapungubwe was already in a state of decline by the late 13th century. This is due to overpopulation putting too much stress on local resources, a situation that may have been brought to a crisis point by a series of droughts.

Yet in our earlier example about the Chinese, we highlighted that because they were alert to such things as overpopulation and its consequences, they turned it around by imposing restrictions on childbirths, at the same time using their excess numbers positively, becoming the manufacturing capital of the world.

In the case of Mapungubwe, trade routes may also have shifted northwards as local resources began to run out. Certainly, the kingdoms that now prospered were to the north, such as Great Zimbabwe, and then the Kingdom of Mutapa in northern Zimbabwe and southern Zambia.

FUTURE-PROOF YOUR CONQUEST

When Europeans 'discovered' the ruins of Mapungubwe in the 19th century CE, just as with those at Great Zimbabwe, they could not believe Africans built such impressive structures.

Theories abounded to somehow explain their presence and confirm racist European beliefs such as attributing them to the ancient Egyptians or Phoenicians. It must be told at this stage that we now know that, that theory is warped because the ancient Phoenicians and Egyptians were black Africans anyway.

Archaeology, however, has since proven that indigenous peoples indeed built both sites in the medieval period. As a result, many of the artefacts from Mapungubwe can be seen today at the Mapungubwe Museum in Pretoria, South Africa. At the same time, the site itself is protected as part of the Mapungubwe National Park.

These Kingdoms were built and yet never avoided their decline. Instead, they ruled, traded and conquered in their pursuits. Yet, they were not future-proof and couldn't adapt to thrive in emerging dispensations.

There are, however, lessons to be learnt which are noble from these great nations. There is a scripture written about Christ that his Kingdom will know no end.

It is important that you build an empire, but it is equally important that you infuse infinity to that which you build. It is vital that you watch whatever you create against decline, which is a natural phenomenon.

If you leave a piece of iron to the elements, no matter how tough iron is, it will rust and decay and become part of the nature around it. But, if you varnish and polish it daily, it can become itself forever.

11 WALKING ON WATER

Living By Faith

Don't worry, about a thing, 'cause every little thing's, gonna be all right - **Bob Marley**

Robert Nesta Marley, popularly known as Bob Marley, was an icon. He was not just a musical talent, he was a human rights activist, a Pan-Africanist and a legend. Note that there is a difference between an icon and a legend. Bob Marley was both.

He was not just a Reggae regal, but he was also a true prophet of peace and justice, particularly to the disenfranchised. He preached in song that the future of mankind was unsustainable with so much inequality in the world.

He sang his heart out to the world, and oh what a heart! He declared in not so many words that until equilibrium is reached and maintained in the world, there would be continuous unhappiness. Yet he sang, "don't worry about a thing, 'cause everything's gonna be alright." The contradiction in his optimism in the midst of such pessimism is what I want to explore in this chapter.

Like Muhammad Ali the boxer, Marley was more than the audible and visible talent that he was. Like Ali, who was more than a boxer, Marley was more than a musician. Not that those careers and talents are not enough to express oneself and raise one's place in the world singularly.

Rather, it is his transcendence that catches the eye. To transcend yourself or even your talents, that is to *really* live life to its fullness. It is to multiply the ways in which you exist. So, even though he exited our earthly shores while still young, we are still talking, singing and writing about him and the lessons derived.

Bob Marley's optimistic outlook that he preached to the world was amazing, for while he lived, he spread his positivity to the world's downtrodden. He had a way of inspiring people to unlock their happiness and experience a more extraordinary life. He believed that everything will be alright, and that every man has a right to decide his destiny. He spread that kind of positivity in his living years, which is still being spread even after he departed from our shores, an early exist if I might say. People like him could never live long enough anyway.

We have been called to a higher life of great possibilities and to attain life's greater promises. The word 'life' just of itself is full of possibilities. To live is to be, and to be is to stay a possibility as in 'all things are possible to those who be,' especially those who *be-live*. To be alive is to be a possibility and as the sage of old once said, "indeed, it is better to be a living dog than a dead lion."

Do not worry about what to eat, or drink or wear'

It is in the book of Matthew Chapter 6 and verses 34, where Christ says, "Take therefore no thought for the morrow, for the morrow shall take thought for the things of itself. Sufficient unto the day is the evil thereof."

In a previous verse, verse 25, he says, "Therefore I say unto you, take no thought for your life, what ye shall eat and what ye shall drink, nor yet for your body, what ye shall put on. Is not the life more than meat, and the body than raiment?"

In the next verse, he continues, "Behold the fowls of the air, for they sow not, neither do they reap nor gather into barns; yet your heavenly Father feedeth them. Are ye not much better than they?"

Life has to have a better meaning than food, drink and raiment. Ours is to seek a higher calling that transcends thirst, hunger, nakedness and the other tangibles.

Material possessions should find you secure in knowing that each daybreak has been made possible for you to celebrate life. It should be an opportunity and joy to be counted amongst the living, where you still have a moment to make things up. That is what life is – opportunity!

We need to seek first that invisible kingdom, not made by man but God Himself. A domain governed by a superior logic that every little thing, "it's gonna be alright." And only it would be when you embrace that mentality. The 'don't worry about a thing, everything is going to be aright' mentality might sound simplistic and naïve. However, I promise you that it will not only remove creases off your forehead but will also release a whole lot of positive energies that will propel you and your life to places you might never even have dreamt of.

The greater things of life belong to positive spirits. 'Like attracts like' is more than just a maxim.

So don't you worry about a thing. Bob Marley might have been high on weed when he sang that song, but if we need weed to get to that wisdom, then let's have weed. Not worrying about a thing is that important.

When we are anxious, our bodies release a hormone called adrenalin or epinephrine to neutralise our fears. That means that even our physical bodies know that fear is not good for us. If our fears are not managed, they will deny us the happy life we are supposed to lead. The life force of man is driven by the twin forces of fear and faith. Those who fear, lose, and those who have *faith*, win. To win, in this life, you need faith.

"Whatever the difficulty, we have no option but to 'arise and shine.'"

You must therefore believe in God, believe in yourself and believe in your dreams and gifts. Fear will often creep in, but it is just a passing breeze unless you embrace it.

Abraham was awarded righteousness by God only because he believed. Without faith, the Holy Book says, it is impossible to please God. Because of his faith in God, a thing that pleases God so much, the Lord was pleased to call him His friend. Nobody in biblical history ever got that kind of accolade but the one who believed. To be counted amongst the friends of God is a great honour indeed and a great plus.

We all desire to pursue financial freedom for ourselves where our families would be secured. However, faith places us in a permanent place of peace and prosperity. So the transition from fear to faith presents a trajectory that brings personal hope that life will be better.

Yes, like any other journey of life, we go through dark and dangerous valleys, but if they don't kill us, they must make us stronger – and that's when we have confronted our fears with faith.

When there's fear, faith must arise
When there's doubt, hope must emerge
When our eyes cannot see where we are going,
Our souls and our spirits must trust the process, that it is well.

Remember the barren Shunammite woman who asked the prophet, Elijah, for a child and the man of God called the heavens, and she was granted her wish? When that child died, she called on the prophet, who asked if it was well with her.

Is it well with you, is it well with your husband, is it well with your child? He asked. She refused to say anything else except that it was well with her and her husband and her child. And the prophet came to her and prayed for the child to come back to life.

She is the one who has inspired the song by Horatio G Spafford, "It is well with my soul."

When peace, like a river, attendeth my way,

When sorrows like sea billows roll; whatever my lot,

Thou hast taught me to say,

It is well. It is well with my soul.

It is well with my soul, It is well.

It is well with my soul.

Whatever the difficulty, we have no option but to 'arise and shine.' Unlock the little faith that is trapped in you. Fear blows your fortunes away. So feed your faith, and starve your fears.

Forgive yourself and move on

Don't worry about a thing also means don't worry about the past. Forgive the past, your past. No matter what happened yesterday, you need to keep going. At one stage or the other, we all have done silly things with our lives, and you cannot punish yourself forever for burning eggs on a frying pan.

Go look for fresh eggs and have breakfast. Life is too short. When it comes to forgiveness, we have learnt to forgive others, but when it comes to forgiving ourselves, we have faltered. Love your neighbour as you love yourself means first loving yourself. Loving yourself sometimes might just start with forgiving yourself, giving yourself some slack.

It was Bob Marley again who said the 'road of life is rocky and you may stumble too, so while you talk about me, someone else is judging you.' We may have undermined our state, even downtrodden ourselves with guilt, yet we still have a chance to appraise ourselves and remind the man or the woman in that mirror, 'Who is the man?' or 'Who is the woman?'

Promise yourself that your best is yet to come

You must constantly remind yourself that tomorrow is the new daybreak to make a better deal of everything. We can only improve and be the better versions of ourselves.

When we meet people in the morning, we often shower them with goodwill without even realising it. We say to them good morning. When Virgin Mary was greeted by the angel, her social status changed forever. Perhaps before you even say good morning to anyone else, you should say good morning to yourself.

Believe in a renewed life

You must be born anew in how you look at life. Learn to refuel your empty tank. Restore yourself to freshness. It may be just to make yourself a fresh cup of Thai tea. Whatever will invigorate your spirit, that's renewal. The journey is long, and you cannot afford to deplete your strength. Learn to revive your energies and resume a routine that will propel you to freshness.

Dealing with Fear

King David saw many battles in the valley, but he never kept his head down. He had the faith of the little shepherd boy even during his adult life. The Lord is my shepherd. I shall not want always reverberated in his heart. He is famous for saying, 'Though I walk through the valley of the shadow of death, I will fear no evil.' He removed himself from the emotions of the moment; he refused to fear while trudging through valleys, even the valley of the shadow of death which is supposed to be the meanest of valleys in geography.

We bring upon ourselves the limitation to 'own' our emotions as though they were our realities. In his book "Think Like a Monk: Train your mind for peace and purpose every day", Jay Shetty puts a compelling case as to why we should detach ourselves from our fears. We tend to refer to them with a sense of attachment where we become the emotions. He further argues that 'most of our fears are clearly as a result of attachment – our need to own and control things.'

When we are angry, we tend to say, 'I am angry. I am sad. I am afraid.' He concludes that we need to try shifting from 'I am angry to I feel angry' In other words, we should separate our emotions from our beings.

"Those who fear, lose, and those who have *faith*, win."

It is important not to be what you feel because, in life, you will feel many things, but you must still be yourself. You cannot be your feelings.

The reason why people commit suicide is that they become so much what they feel, ultimately they lose themselves in the moment. You are not what you feel; you are who you are. That should be your anchor, especially if you know who you are.

You have to walk through some valley to experience your mountaintop. Some of the greatest books that I have read and movies that I have watched were created by true artists who know life and have two characteristics about them, valleys and mountains.

What can one say about Alexander Dumas's The Count of Monte Christo, and what can you say about the Shawshank Redemption? Valleys and mountains, climbing up and down to one's destiny.

I remember a rhyme that we used to reside in kindergarten.

London town.
This is the way to London town,
One foot up and one foot down,
Oh, this is the way to London town.

At that time in my growing up, London was the imperial capital of the world, and there was only one way to get there, one foot in the valley and one foot on the mountain, one foot up and one foot down, that was the only way.

I must say a stupid colonial rhyme, but hey, it is handy for my purposes here. I don't even know what the person who wrote that little rhyme wanted to tell the world.

Life at the mountaintop teaches us to appreciate that there's more to life than what we see. There is more power, more grace and more strength in this life than we often think when we are in the valley.

Life has a way of offering us more, yet we don't always see. Mountaintop experiences are good for motivation. When there, you must breathe in and savour the moment and expand your dreams. Whilst still at the mountain top, enjoy the view and vantage point, for you are there only for a moment. Breathe in and gather your strength so that the next valley will not destroy you. Be like King David and say 'though I walk through the valley... I will fear no evil.'

Whoever you are, you must know that your destiny is more important than your circumstances.

WHEN THE SUN SETS

There are times when the sun sets on us, and the journey is still long, yet when you have tasted victory before, you know that the sun will rise again. It shall be morning again. When the sun has set, and it's dark, lie low.

Staying up may not bring the brightness of day, but nightmares and misery. Isn't it so true what Kim says that 'our faith can move mountains, but our doubts can create them'? Such paradoxes.

Sometimes instead of moving mountains, we create them. Most of the things we fear would never happen, but the fear is so real that sometimes we experience the unreal as real, and we suffer unnecessarily.

The sun does often set, but it always rises again, and that is guaranteed. It sounds very much like little futile knowledge, yet it is an essential tool to put in your toolbox so you can be able to handle the vicissitudes of this life.

We shouldn't worry about tomorrow when today is done right.'

Dale Carnegie used to say, 'remember, today is the tomorrow you worried about yesterday' and how accurate that is. Our lives' journeys are a sum total of our today's doings.

No one knows the texture of tomorrow. So we shouldn't worry

about a strip of time that has not yet been visited upon us. However, we need to do right today so that tomorrow can take care of itself.

Life is made up of times and seasons and how we spend the next hour is very crucial. It then becomes increasingly significant that we spend our time wisely.

One great scenario planner, Clem Sunter, devoted his time during the transition into the arrival of the millennium by putting a masterpiece of work. He entitled it, "Never mind the millennium; what about the next 24 hours?"

In his scenario work, Sunter argues that while many would be pre-occupied and concentrating on predictions for the next thousand years, one needs to concern himself with the here and now.

Devoting oneself to a higher calling requires that one be fully present and genuinely engaged daily. This is an altruistic form of living, and in that, there lays our philosophy of serving.

The important matter is never to chase shadows and darkness. On the contrary, each day, our lives should enlighten others. We should treat darkness as merely the absence of light. 'It is better to light up the candle than to curse the darkness', as W.L Watkinson would aptly say.

A new day must beckon for you to realise your miracle, placing faith into a winning streak. This requires a pepping up of your spirit each day. We need to grow through all our experiences. Everyone must craft a practical approach to distil our lives from any clutter. There is darkness around and everywhere, and the discerning spirit will find the light.

Build to last, knowing that tomorrow should be a little better than today. So when today is done right, we shouldn't worry about tomorrow. For tomorrow is nothing but the sum total of today's thoughts and actions. Therefore, do not worry about tomorrow; we need to concern ourselves with the present, the moment before us.

Tackle today, and today will tackle tomorrow. Plant the seed today and the harvest you will worry about tomorrow. As the inspiring wisdom found in this old Chinese proverb would say, "The best time to plant a tree was 20 years ago. The second best time is now."

Many are still to leverage on the growth opportunities, albeit when 'the now' is deferred, nothing manifests in the future. Now is a good time to start. Now is a good time to act. With whatever you have, that too is good enough to get you started.

Avoid being part of the *late.com* generation. A generation that postpones and postpones and postpones. Yesterday is gone, today is here for the taking, and tomorrow is only possible because we learned from yesterday and took action today.∎

12 THE MOUNTAIN TOP

Being Courageous

"I have walked that long road to freedom. I have tried not to falter; I have made missteps along the way. But I have discovered the secret that after climbing a great hill, one only finds that there are many more hills to climb. I have taken a moment here to rest, to steal a view of the glorious vista that surrounds me, to look back on the distance I have come. But I can only rest for a moment, for with freedom come responsibilities, and I dare not linger, for my long walk is not ended." - **Nelson Mandela**

Nelson Mandela is not just a hero to many, but he was a prophet of peace who lifted the spirit of humanity across many worlds to its highest creed. He was the godfather of global politics who taught us that with every freedom, there should come responsibility. For one to experience a mountaintop, know that there are always many other hills that would need to be climbed and valleys too that would need to be traversed.

So whilst you are still on top of the hill, remember that the walk is still long. It's always a long walk to true freedom. There are ups and downs to life, any life, and it is the ability and the fortitude to trudge through those that ultimately make successful individuals.

There is no need for me to promise you falsities; life is just like that. But you cannot get to the mountain top without the act of climbing, and climbing is not as effortless as sliding. A lot goes into such an effort.

Vince Lombardi places the importance of this matter of being on the mountain top by saying, 'the man on top of the mountain didn't just fall there.'

The late Vince Lombardi is considered by many to be the greatest coach in American football history. He is recognised as one of the greatest coaches and leaders in the history of all American sports.

Falling is effortless; climbing, on the other hand, takes a lot of effort and a straining of muscle and sinew. To get to the mountain top is in the action of climbing.

In earnest, the larger part of our life is truly lived in the valley, not at the mountaintop. And I am not saying this in a negative way because if you are a warrior, you should enjoy the valley as much as the mountain top.

The battles we wage, the challenges we face, all are fought on our way to the mountaintop, but that does not mean the valley is a gloomy place. *On the contrary, the valley* and the valley of the shadow of death are a totally different story.

Your attitude will determine how you feel. But I will tell you this: there are very few people on the mountain top. It's all shaped like a pyramid. Sadly, life is a pyramid scheme.

King David's 'though I walk through the valley of the shadow of death' is abandonment to reality. It means that he has been able to find joy and fearlessness in the harsh realities of this life and its vicissitudes.

On the hill, we go for inspiration and to forecast what lies ahead at the valley. If you are grown like me, you've had to go through the death of a loved one, a mother, a father, a brother, sometimes even a child. It is part of life, and you have to tuck in and move on. Such is life.

Mountaintop experiences are for joy but also for exploration. So we spend nervy moments walking through the 'valley', and we occasionally take a moment to have a better view of things up the mountain. And when you get to these mountaintop experiences, drink in every drop of them, enjoy them thoroughly and greedily, for they are needful to give you strength for the next moment.

Then, we return to fight the battles at the valley where the real action occurs. Learn to love the valleys, learn not to fear them. King David says in the famous Psalm 23, and I am willing to repeat it over and over again,

"Though I walk through the valley of the shadow of death, I will fear no evil, for thou art with me. Thy rod and thy staff, they comfort me."

It is that kind of faith that sustained him, and it should sustain you too. "Surely goodness and mercy shall follow me all the days of my life" is the kind of faith you should take into your life. With that kind of belief, I guarantee you that you will make good, no matter what. If you have no fear in the valley of the shadow of death, then your life is good.

In other words, all I can say is that with the proper attitude, all life is good. 'Surely goodness and mercy shall follow me all the days of my life' says a lot about a man and his trust in God.

Some of the strongest people I have met in my life are people who do not fear hunger and death. They can venture into entrepreneurship and risk hunger while pushing ideas that the world has not yet bought into. Unfortunately, fearfulness is what makes men just too careful, and careful society does not achieve much in this world.

I have not heard in my life of a careful man who ever made any stride in this life. I invited a friend into an entrepreneurial venture that would have demanded him to quit his job, and he said to me, "I can't," and I asked why, and he said I am afraid of hunger.

This dear brother lost out because he could not handle tomorrow's possible hunger, which is not even guaranteed.

Saul and the Israelites assembled and camped in the Valley of Elah and drew up their battle line to meet the Philistines. Prophet Samuel chronicles this day in the 17th Chapter of his first book. 'The Philistines occupied one hill and the Israelites another, with the valley in between.' David, the man who fought a bear and a lion in the wilderness and triumphed, won the battle that day for the Israelites.

The lion and the bear were very tough man-eating occasions, but they were training moments for the young warrior. Thinking about it, he could have become feed 'specially for the lion, but he fought through those experiences and gained strength, also earning mental trophies.

Those are the valleys of the shadow of death that prepared David for the next battle. The battle with the most feared champion of the Philistines, a vulgar and arrogant man who spoke to the Israelis as he pleased, emasculating their king and desecrating their God. David comes and says, 'Who is this foul creature who even has the guts to speak ill of the God of Israel?'

"Mountaintop experiences are for joy but also for exploration."

They say to him, "his name is Goliath, and we are going to suffer his verbal abuse for no one in our ranks is willing to take him on." They give him Goliath's CV, which they all think is very impressive, but the son of Jesse is not impressed in the least.

Didn't the good book say, "the people that know their God shall be strong and do exploits"? By me, even if young David had failed to kill Goliath or was killed by Goliath, he would still be my hero.

Which valley has prepared you for battle? Valleys are lows in geography, but they exist in the geography of our lives too. Nobody is going to live their entire life on the mountain top.

Even Christ Jesus had his Golgotha, Lord Moses had his wilderness, and Joseph had his pit and prison, so did Nelson Mandela. So to think that you could go through life forever on the top of mountains and hills and achieve greatness by that is simply being naïve.

I have read many biographies and the common thread in all epic stories is that the greats of all times are only great or only became great because they survived the valleys and gained their strength there while others faltered.

If you are great and your God is greater, you should be strong enough to survive and thrive in all terrains. The good book says, "even the young lions do go hungry and suffer hunger, but those that trust upon the Lord shall renew their strength, they shall mount up with wings like eagles, they shall run and never faint." That is what I am talking about 'running and never fainting.'

WORKING YOUR WAY TO THE TOP

Actually, 'where is the whole world?' This was Elon Musk's existential question since he was a child. Have you ever cared to ask, 'where is the world,' 'where is your life,' 'where are you headed to?' To the valley, or the mountain top or perhaps a bit of both? The truth is you should aim for the mountain top and accept the valleys as part of the path but not as a destiny. The valley may be part of your journey, but it is undoubtedly not your destiny

At the time of publishing this book, Elon Musk, a South African born dollar billionaire, is on top of the world rankings as one of the richest man on earth. His father, Errol, proudly shared a moving story with Forbes that 'the kind of things he would come up with as a youngster were always surprising.' For example, when he was very small, he would ask me, 'where is the whole world.' His dad would call him a 'Genius Boy', which he later proved by becoming a genius man.

Yet as the story goes, 'despite his remarkable talent and

comfortable upbringing, Musk's childhood was blighted with peculiar challenges. As the shortest, smallest and smartest kid in class, he was an easy target for bullies who tormented him until he was 15 years old.' And when his parents divorced in 1980, it was the final straw to break the camel's back. But that camel's back stayed intact.

It has never been easy to climb to the top, and oftentimes circumstances around one make it difficult to continue trudging on. Climbing has never been a child's play, but passion overcomes the aching muscles and the persistent whisper that says 'quit, it isn't worth your while.' Yet again, when you win this first round of difficulties, the aching muscles, you are spurred to move on further.

Such, it was, with Elon. He was shaped by so many of these stumbling blocks to becoming what he became. And alas, he's on top of the mountain, and now his eyes are on Mars.

Mountains are no longer a challenge to him.

He is looking up higher.

Elon Reeve Musk is now an international entrepreneur and business magnate. He is the founder, CEO, and chief engineer at SpaceX. He is an early-stage investor, CEO, and product architect of Tesla, Inc. He founded The Boring Company and co-founded Neuralink and OpenAI. A centibillionaire, Musk is one of the wealthiest people in the world. The little boy who asked the difficult questions has now got them answered throughout his life. He wanted to know where the rest of the world was, and he found it all by himself.

As it has been noticed throughout his pioneering journey, his work ethic and hard work remained the cornerstone of his entrepreneurial ethos.

The story of Elon Musk is the story of all of us. In Jesus' parables, most of the time, he began with this assertion, "There was once a man who...Our story, your story, is the story of a man who...." So I bring stories of men in this writ, men who succeeded despite odds, to say that if others could do it, so can you.

So, there was a man, a woman, and then there is you. You are the reason why I wrote this book, and you are the one that must make the words of this book alive through your own life and application.

Every time I tell you a story of a man or a woman who was able to achieve this or that, I am challenging you. I am saying that since you are no different from these people, what exactly are you waiting for?

MOUNTAINS DON'T GROW, BUT WE DO

A certain man sojourned to the summit of Mt. Everest. He was still young. His first attempt to the loftiest of summits was returned with failure and disappointment, as he failed terribly to scale that gargantuan. His name was Edward Hillary. So he looked at Mt. Everest and said to it, "mountain, you don't grow, but I grow. I will return to conquer you." Well, didn't Christ admonish us to speak to mountains?

A few years later, Sir Edward Hillary returned with a crew and successfully submitted Mt. Everest together with *Tenzing Norgay*. The twain became the first two men in recorded history to ever do so.

Edmund Percival Hillary was a New Zealand mountaineer, explorer, and philanthropist. On 29 May 1953, Hillary and Sherpa mountaineer Tenzing Norgay became the first climbers confirmed to have reached the summit of Mount Everest.

They were part of the ninth British expedition to Everest led by John Hunt. From 1985 to 1988, he served as New Zealand's High Commissioner to India and Bangladesh and concurrently as Ambassador to Nepal.

Hillary became interested in mountaineering while in secondary school. He did his first major climb in 1939, reaching the summit of Mount Olivier. The desire to climb is a very great thing.

Sometimes all you need is help from others.

No mountain climber is an ordinary person. While people chill in flatlands, why would anyone aspire to climb mountains? He served in the Royal New Zealand Air Force as a navigator during World War II and was wounded in an accident. Before the Everest expedition, Hillary had been part of the British reconnaissance expedition to the mountain in 1951 and an unsuccessful attempt to climb Cho Oyu in 1952.

As part of the Commonwealth Trans-Antarctic Expedition, he reached the South Pole overland in 1958. He subsequently reached the North Pole, making him the first person to reach both poles and one of the first two to summit Everest.

"Time Magazine" named him one of the 100 most influential people of the 20th century.

Following his ascent of Everest, Hillary devoted himself to assisting the Sherpa people of Nepal through the Himalayan Trust, which he established. His efforts are credited with the construction of many schools and hospitals in Nepal. Hillary had numerous honours conferred upon him, including the Order of the Garter in 1995. Upon his death in 2008, he was given a state funeral in New Zealand.

Sometimes we need to address our conditions and impediments and face them with greater determination and equanimity. That's growth, and such an attitude to move mountains and build empires is vital in this world. This man refused to give up just because, for one moment, the mountain conquered him. Instead, he spoke to the mountain and said, "mountain, I will be back."

That is the spirit of a conqueror and the heart of an empire builder. Our problems are not insurmountable. They can be conquered. They often look so, but as you know, looks can be deceiving. However, we will need a concerted effort to address them.

Sometimes all you need is help from others. There are so many people in the world that can and will help you in the path towards your success; yet again, whether you will succeed or fail is entirely your personal responsibility. Others can help you climb a stair but not entirely to achieve success.

FINDING YOUR FREQUENCY

We all have this one unique thing, and that distinguishes us from others, our unique selling proposition. Discover that for yourself. Discover your dream life, raise your power and find your frequency.

Find that thing that is unique to yourself because it is there, whoever you are. Then, when you apply some of the principles that I am going to nail down to you, soon you will discover that which makes you tick. Let me enumerate them to you, can I?.

Discipline: Doing the same thing, the right thing with greater effort and relentlessness. Decide what your life-work is, and don't let go. I know a man with the greatest ideas. He will start to grow, but the next time you meet him, he has a new idea, and he has abandoned the one he so enthusiastically shared with you a year ago.

Dedication: We have to learn that no life grows excellent unless it is thoroughly dedicated & focused. Dedication is following on winning routines whether you feel to do so or not.

Dominance: In Africa, every day, a lion wakes up and chooses to run faster than an antelope. This is for survival, or else it will die of hunger. So work towards dominance in your field of endeavour. The slow and lazy don't get to see the next day in the jungle, only the fast and furious.

Design a growing future: Every future can be designed. In this life, you either emerge as bitter or better. So a shoe mustn't tell afoot how far it can grow. Instead, you must have a design, in other words, a strategic and artistic plan of where you want to be in such and such a time in your life.

Daring: We have to continue to live on the edge where life happens. Nothing in life is accidental, for we all have to take chances and learn to leverage opportunities life brings.

We need to keep growing and keep moving. We must refuse to be steered out of our pursuit. Being ordinary is genuinely out of fashion.

Falling is a given; it happens but if you have to fall— fall forward. Another thing is, make rising up after a fall just as certain as falling is. Shake the dust off of you and rise up after every fall.

The falls will be depending on how far to Mount Everest's peak you are determined to reach. If you want to live your life in the valley, there will be very little falling, but who wants to live their lives in the valley? I hope you don't.

Wrestle until you win.

Often in life, one has to wrestle. Sometimes circumstance is squared against you, but that does not mean that you are the underdog because you can fight back.

I am not a big fan of the sports of wrestling ever since it became *commercialized* and faked, but there is one thing that you can appreciate about the sport, every man who goes into that arena is determined to do everything in their power to win the wrestle.

That is a great attitude that you can take into your life. You can say to yourself, 'I am not in this to lose. In the world of yeses and no's, I am not taking no for an answer. Never.'

When our flaws fail us

You may have flaws, live anxiously and sometimes get angry, but never forget that your life is the biggest enterprise in the world. And you can keep it from going down or bankrupt. Your flaws may stick out but tuck them in and forgive them, and stay cheerful.

Many people out there admire and cheer for you, and this must give you courage. Drink those moments in and keep a happy spirit.

I wish that you always remember that being happy is not having a sky without storms, paths without accidents, work without fatigue, relationships without disappointments.

Being happy is finding strength in forgiveness, hope in battles, security in fear, love in disagreements. Being happy is not only appreciating the smiles but reflecting on the sadness. It is not just celebrating success but also learning lessons from failures.

It is not only having joy in applause but finding joy in sadness.

Being happy is recognising that life is worth living, despite all the challenges, misunderstandings and periods of crises.

Being happy is refusing to be a victim of the problems but bending the story of your life and becoming an author of history itself. It is crossing deserts outside of yourself and being able to find yourself an oasis in the secret of your soul.

Being happy is thanking God every morning for the miracle of the life bestowed upon you.

Being happy is not being afraid of your own feelings. It's knowing how to talk to yourself. It's the courage to hear a "No" and be confident enough to receive criticism, although sometimes untrue. Being happy, is to let the child living within us to live freely, happily and simply.

It is having the needed maturity to say, "I was wrong."

It is having the essential courage to say, "forgive me."

It is having the indispensable sensibility to say, "I need you."

It is being able to say, "I love you."

It is having the humility of receptivity.

I want your life to be a hotbed of opportunities and that you be ecstatically happy — and when you go astray to have the courage to start again. This way, you will find that being happy is not having a perfect life but often using your tears to irrigate tolerance and using losses to refine patience.

Using failures to reach that praying moment.

Using obstacles to open the windows of intelligence.

To never giving up hope.

To never giving up on the people you love no matter what they would have done...

To never giving up on being happy because life is a no-miss obstacle, even if it gives you dozens of reasons to demonstrate the contrary.

Stones on the way? I keep them all for one day, I will build a castle from which I will rule my world.▪

13 DULY CHOSEN
Your Seat of Greatness

There are some men who lift the age they inhabit, till all men walk on higher ground in that lifetime. - **Maxwell Anderson**,

I was born in Soweto. Well, no one chooses where you are born, in the main, but the Universe does. I am a middle child, which earned me the responsibility of being the "glue" that holds everything together.

My full name is *Vusumuzi*, which simply means "the one who builds." Throughout my life, I've built. When my eyes opened up to the real world, I was introduced to the harshness and the difficulties that get visited upon children of a working-class family. My father, George, was the hardest working man I've ever known. Since I knew my dad, he's always kept two jobs: an artisan in an industrial engineering firm and an entrepreneur.

My mother, Margareth, was a beautiful lady inside and out.

She was conjoined to my dad early in her life and took up the responsibility of being a caregiver to all my siblings.

The greatness I observed in my dad was that of hard work and providing for us. He was also my real first teacher. The greatness of my mother was in how she served. She served my father directly and indirectly by caring for us and raising us. The twain showed us the two sides of the coin of greatness, as the Chinese would put it, the *ying* and the *yang*.

As I go towards the end of this book, I would like to travel you to a place and time a little over two thousand years ago.

No, let me rather travel you to Sunday, 4 February 1968, and Martin Luther King Jr, who I earlier on mentioned as the most significant influence in my life, is preaching on an event that occasioned over two thousand years ago. As I was going through his speech again after several years, I wanted to quote portions of it in the book, but it was futile. So I decided to borrow the entire sermon since I cannot improve on it.

I also fear that I could harm and not do justice to this great oration through abbreviation and compression. So I am going to let Dr King inspire you in this dying chapter of the book.

The Drum Major Instinct

Our text for the morning is taken from a very familiar passage in the tenth chapter as recorded by Saint Mark. Beginning with the thirty-fifth verse of that chapter, we read these words: "And James and John, the sons of Zebedee, came unto him saying, 'Master, we would that thou shouldest do for us whatsoever we shall desire.' And he said unto them, 'What would ye that I should do for you?' And they said unto him, 'Grant unto us that we may sit, one on thy right hand, and the other on thy left hand, in thy glory.' But Jesus said unto them, 'Ye know not what ye ask: Can ye drink of the cup that I drink of? and be baptized with the baptism that I am baptized with?' And they said unto him, 'We can.' And Jesus said unto them, 'Ye shall indeed drink of the cup that I drink of, and with the baptism that I am baptized withal shall ye be baptized: but to sit on my right hand and on my left hand is not mine to give; but it shall be given to them for whom it is prepared.'" And then Jesus goes on toward the end of that passage to say, "But so shall it not be among you: but whosoever will be great among you, shall be your servant: and whosoever of you will be the chiefest, shall be servant of all."

The setting is clear. James and John are making a specific request of the master. They had dreamed, as most of the Hebrews dreamed, of a coming king of Israel who would set Jerusalem free and establish his kingdom on Mount Zion, and in righteousness rule the world. And they thought of Jesus as this kind of king. And they were thinking of that day when Jesus would reign supreme as this new king of Israel. And they were saying, "Now when you establish your kingdom, let one of us sit on the right hand and the other on the left hand of your throne."

Now very quickly, we would automatically condemn James and John, and we would say they were selfish. Why would they make such a selfish request? But before we condemn them too quickly, let us look calmly and honestly at ourselves, and we will discover that we too have those same basic desires for recognition, for importance. That same desire for attention, that same desire to be first. Of course, the other disciples got mad with James and John, and you could understand why, but we must understand that we have some of the same James and John qualities. And there is deep down within all of us an instinct. It's a kind of drum major instinct—a desire to be out front, a desire to lead the parade, a desire to be first. And it is something that runs the whole gamut of life.

And so before we condemn them, let us see that we all have the drum major instinct. We all want to be important, to surpass others, to achieve distinction, to lead the parade. Alfred Adler, the great psychoanalyst, contends that this is the dominant impulse. Sigmund Freud used to contend that sex was the dominant impulse, and Adler came with a new argument saying that this quest for recognition, this desire for attention, this desire for distinction is the basic impulse, the basic drive of human life, this drum major instinct.

And you know, we begin early to ask life to put us first. Our first cry as a baby was a bid for attention. And all through childhood the drum major impulse or instinct is a major obsession. Children ask life to grant them first place. They are a little bundle of ego. And they have innately the drum major impulse or the drum major instinct.

Now in adult life, we still have it, and we really never get by it. We like to do something good. And you know, we like to be praised for it. Now if you don't believe that, you just go on living life, and you will discover very soon that you like to be praised. Everybody likes it, as a matter of fact. And somehow *this warm glow we feel when we are praised or when our name is in print is something of the vitamin A to our ego. Nobody is unhappy when they are praised, even if they know they don't deserve it and even if they don't believe it. The only unhappy people about praise is when that praise is going too much toward somebody else. (That's right) But everybody likes to be praised because of this real drum major instinct.*

Now the presence of the drum major instinct is why so many people are "joiners." You know, there are some people who just join everything. And it's really a quest for attention and recognition and importance. And they get names that give them that impression. So you get your groups, and they become the "Grand Patron," and the little fellow who is henpecked at home needs a chance to be the "Most Worthy of the Most Worthy" of something. It is the drum major impulse and longing that runs the gamut of human life. And so we see it everywhere, this quest for recognition. And we join things, over-join really, that we think that we will find that recognition in.

Now the presence of this instinct explains why we are so often taken by advertisers. You know, those gentlemen of massive verbal persuasion. And they have a way of saying things to you that kind of gets you into buying. In order to be a man of distinction, you must drink this whiskey. In order to make your neighbors envious, you must drive this type of car. (Make it plain) In order to be lovely to love you must wear this kind of lipstick or this kind of perfume. And you know, before you know it, you're just buying that stuff. (Yes) That's the way the advertisers do it.

I got a letter the other day, and it was a new magazine coming out. And it opened up, "Dear Dr. King: As you know, you are on many mailing lists. And you are categorized as highly intelligent, progressive, a lover of the arts and the sciences, and I know you will want to read what I have to say." Of course I did. After you said all of that and explained me so exactly, of course I wanted to read it. [laughter]

But very seriously, it goes through life; the drum major instinct is real. (Yes) And you know what else it causes to happen? It often causes us to live above our means. (Make it plain) It's nothing but the drum major instinct. Do you ever see people buy cars that they can't even begin to buy in terms of their income? (Amen) [laughter] You've seen people riding around in Cadillacs and Chryslers who don't earn enough to have a good T-Model Ford. (Make it plain) But it feeds a repressed ego.

You know, economists tell us that your automobile should not cost more than half of your annual income. So if you make an income of five thousand dollars, your car shouldn't cost more than about twenty-five hundred. That's just good economics. And if it's a family of two, and both members of the family make ten thousand dollars, they would have to make out with one car. That would be good economics, although it's often inconvenient. But so often, haven't you seen people making five thousand dollars a year and driving a car that costs six thousand? And they wonder why their ends never meet. [laughter] That's a fact.

Now the economists also say that your house shouldn't

cost—if you're buying a house, it shouldn't cost more than twice your income. That's based on the economy and how you would make ends meet. So, if you have an income of five thousand dollars, it's kind of difficult in this society. But say it's a family with an income of ten thousand dollars, the house shouldn't cost much more than twenty thousand. Well, I've seen folk making ten thousand dollars, living in a forty-and fifty-thousand-dollar house. And you know they just barely make it. They get a check every month somewhere, and they owe all of that out before it comes in. Never have anything to put away for rainy days.

But now the problem is, it is the drum major instinct. And you know, you see people over and over again with the drum major instinct taking them over. And they just live their lives trying to outdo the Joneses. (Amen) They got to get this coat because this particular coat is a little better and a little better-looking than Mary's coat. And I got to drive this car because it's something about this car that makes my car a little better than my neighbor's car. (Amen) I know a man who used to live in a thirty-five-thousand-dollar house. And other people started building thirty-five-thousand-dollar houses, so he built a seventy-five-thousand-dollar house. And then somebody else built a seventy-five-thousand-dollar house, and he built a hundred-thousand-dollar house. And I don't know where he's going to end up if he's going to live his life trying to keep up with the Joneses.

There comes a time that the drum major instinct can become destructive. (Make it plain) And that's where I want to move now. I want to move to the point of saying that if *this instinct is not harnessed, it becomes a very dangerous, pernicious instinct. For instance, if it isn't harnessed, it causes one's personality to become distorted. I guess that's the most damaging aspect of it: what it does to the personality. If it isn't harnessed, you will end up day in and day out trying to deal with your ego problem by boasting. Have you ever heard people that—you know, and I'm sure you've met them—that really become sickening because they just sit up all the time talking about themselves. (Amen) And they just boast and boast and boast, and that's the person who has not harnessed the drum major instinct.*

And then it does other things to the personality. It causes you to lie about who you know sometimes. (Amen, Make it plain) There are some people who are influence peddlers. And in their attempt to deal with the drum major instinct, they have to try to identify with the so-called big-name people. (Yeah, Make it plain) And if you're not careful, they will make you think they know somebody that they don't really know. (Amen) They know them well, they sip tea with them, and they this-and-that. That happens to people.

And the other thing is that it causes one to engage ultimately in activities that are merely used to get attention. Criminologists tell us that some people are driven to crime because of this drum major instinct. They don't feel that they are getting enough attention through the normal channels of social behavior, and so they turn to anti-social behavior in order to get attention, in order to feel important. (Yeah) And so they get that gun, and before they know it they robbed a bank in a quest for recognition, in a quest for importance.

And then the final great tragedy of the distorted personality is the fact that when one fails to harness this instinct, (Glory to God) he ends up trying to push others down in order to push himself up. (Amen) And whenever you do that, you engage in some of the most vicious activities. You will spread evil, vicious, lying gossip on people, because you are trying to pull them down in order to push yourself up. (Make it plain) And the great issue of life is to harness the drum major instinct.

Now the other problem is, when you don't harness the drum major instinct—this uncontrolled aspect of it—is that it leads to snobbish exclusivism. It leads to snobbish exclusivism. (Make it plain) And you know, this is the danger of social clubs and fraternities—I'm in a fraternity; I'm in two or three—for sororities and all of these, I'm not talking against them. I'm saying it's the danger. The danger is that they can become forces of classism and exclusivism where somehow you get a degree of satisfaction because you are in something exclusive. And that's fulfilling something, you know—that I'm in this fraternity, and it's the best fraternity in the world, and everybody can't get in this fraternity. So it ends up, you know, a very exclusive kind of thing.

And you know, that can happen with the church; I know churches get in that bind sometimes. (Amen, Make it plain) I've been to churches, you know, and they say, "We have so many doctors, and so many school teachers, and so many lawyers, and so many businessmen in our church." And that's fine, because doctors need to go to church, and lawyers, and businessmen, teachers—they ought to be in church. But they say that—even the preacher sometimes will go all through *that—they say that as if the other people don't count. (Amen)*

And the church is the one place where a doctor ought to forget that he's a doctor. The church is the one place where a Ph.D. ought to forget that he's a Ph.D. (Yes) The church is the one place that the school teacher ought to forget the degree she has behind her name. The church is the one place where the lawyer ought to forget that he's a lawyer. And any church that violates the "whosoever will, let him come" doctrine is a dead, cold church, (Yes) and nothing but a little social club with a thin veneer of religiosity.

When the church is true to its nature, (Whoo) it says, "Whosoever will, let him come." (Yes) And it does not supposed to satisfy the perverted uses of the drum major instinct. It's the one place where everybody should be the same, standing before a common master and savior. (Yes, sir) And a recognition grows out of this—that all men are brothers because they are children (Yes) of a common father.

The drum major instinct can lead to exclusivism in one's thinking and can lead one to feel that because he has some training, he's a little better than that person who doesn't have it. Or because he has some economic security, that he's a little better than that person who doesn't have it. And that's the uncontrolled, perverted use of the drum major instinct.

Now the other thing is, that it leads to tragic—and we've seen it happen so often—tragic race prejudice. Many who have written about this problem—Lillian Smith used to say it beautifully in some of her books. And she would say it to the point of getting men and women to see the source of the problem. Do you know that a lot of the race problem grows out of the drum major instinct? A need that some people have to feel superior. A need that some people have to feel that they are first, and to feel that their white skin ordained them to be first. (Make it plain, today, 'cause I'm against it, so help me God) And they have said over and over again in ways that we see with our own eyes.

In fact, not too long ago, a man down in Mississippi said that God was a charter member of the White Citizens Council. And so God being the charter member means that everybody who's in that has a kind of divinity, a kind of superiority. And think of what has happened in history as a result of this perverted use of the drum major instinct. It has led to the most tragic prejudice, the most tragic expressions of man's inhumanity to man.

The other day I was saying, I always try to do a little converting when I'm in jail. And when we were in jail in Birmingham the other day, the white wardens and all enjoyed coming around the cell to talk about the race problem. And they were showing us where we were so wrong demonstrating. And they were showing us where segregation was so right.

And they were showing us where intermarriage was so wrong. So I would get to preaching, and we would get to talking—calmly, because they wanted to talk about it. And then we got down one day to the point—that was the second or third day—to talk about where they lived, and how much they were earning. And when those brothers told me what they were earning, I said, "Now, you know what? You ought to be

*marching with us. [laughter] You're just as poor as Negroes."
And I said, "You are put in the position of supporting your
oppressor, because through prejudice and blindness, you fail
to see that the same forces that oppress Negroes in American
society oppress poor white people. (Yes) And all you are living
on is the satisfaction of your skin being white, and the drum
major instinct of thinking that you are somebody big because
you are white. And you're so poor you can't send your children
to school. You ought to be out here marching with every one of
us every time we have a march."*

*Now that's a fact. That the poor white has been put into
this position, where through blindness and prejudice, (Make
it plain) he is forced to support his oppressors. And the only
thing he has going for him is the false feeling that he's superior
because his skin is white—and can't hardly eat and make his
ends meet week in and week out. (Amen)*

*And not only does this thing go into the racial struggle, it
goes into the struggle between nations. And I would submit
to you this morning that what is wrong in the world today is
that the nations of the world are engaged in a bitter, colossal
contest for supremacy. And if something doesn't happen to
stop this trend, I'm sorely afraid that we won't be here to talk
about Jesus Christ and about God and about brotherhood too
many more years. (Yeah)*

*If somebody doesn't bring an end to this suicidal thrust that
we see in the world today, none of us are going to be around,
because somebody's going to make the mistake through our
senseless blunderings of dropping a nuclear bomb somewhere.*

And then another one is going to drop. And don't let anybody fool you, this can happen within a matter of seconds. (Amen) They have twenty-megaton bombs in Russia right now that can destroy a city as big as New York in three seconds, with everybody wiped away, and every building. And we can do the same thing to Russia and China.

But this is why we are drifting. And we are drifting there because nations are caught up with the drum major instinct. "I must be first." "I must be supreme." "Our nation must rule the world." (Preach it) And I am sad to say that the nation in which we live is the supreme culprit. And I'm going to continue to say it to America, because I love this country too much to see the drift that it has taken.

God didn't call America to do what she's doing in the world now. (Preach it, preach it) God didn't call America to engage in a senseless, unjust war as the war in Vietnam. And we are criminals in that war. We've committed more war crimes almost than any nation in the world, and I'm going to continue to say it. And we won't stop it because of our pride and our arrogance as a nation.

But God has a way of even putting nations in their place. (Amen) The God that I worship has a way of saying, "Don't play with me." (Yes) He has a way of saying, as the God of the Old Testament used to say to the Hebrews, "Don't play with me, Israel. Don't play with me, Babylon. (Yes) Be still and know that I'm God. And if you don't stop your reckless course, I'll rise up and break the backbone of your power." (Yes) And that can happen to America. (Yes)

Every now and then I go back and read Gibbons' Decline and Fall of the Roman Empire. And when I come and look at America, I say to myself, the parallels are frightening. And we have perverted the drum major instinct.

But let me rush on to my conclusion, because I want you to see what Jesus was really saying. What was the answer that Jesus gave these men? It's very interesting.

One would have thought that Jesus would have condemned them. One would have thought that Jesus would have said, "You are out of your place. You are selfish. Why would you raise such a question?"

But that isn't what Jesus did; he did something altogether different. He said in substance, "Oh, I see, you want to be first. You want to be great. You want to be important. You want to be significant. Well, you ought to be. If you're going to be my disciple, you must be." But he reordered priorities. And he said, "Yes, don't give up this instinct. It's a good instinct if you use it right. (Yes)

It's a good instinct if you don't distort it and pervert it. Don't give it up. Keep feeling the need for being important. Keep feeling the need for being first. But I want you to be first in love. (Amen) I want you to be first in moral excellence. I want you to be first in generosity. That is what I want you to do."

And he transformed the situation by giving a new definition of greatness. And you know how he said it? He said, "Now brethren, I can't give you greatness. And really, I can't make you first." This is what Jesus said to James and John. "You must earn it.

True greatness comes not by favoritism, but by fitness. And the right hand and the left are not mine to give, they belong to those who are prepared." (Amen)

And so Jesus gave us a new norm of greatness. If you want to be important—wonderful. If you want to be recognized—wonderful. If you want to be great—wonderful. But recognize that he who is greatest among you shall be your servant. (Amen) That's a new definition of greatness.

And this morning, the thing that I like about it: by giving that definition of greatness, it means that everybody can be great, (Everybody) because everybody can serve. (Amen) You don't have to have a college degree to serve. (All right) You don't have to make your subject and your verb agree to serve. You don't have to know about Plato and Aristotle to serve. You don't have to know Einstein's theory of relativity to serve. You don't have to know the second theory of thermodynamics in physics to serve. (Amen) You only need a heart full of grace, (Yes, sir, Amen) a soul generated by love. (Yes) And you can be that servant.

I know a man—and I just want to talk about him a minute, and maybe you will discover who I'm talking about as I go down the way (Yeah) because he was a great one. And he just went about serving. He was born in an obscure village, (Yes, sir) the child of a poor peasant woman. And then he grew up in still another obscure village, where he worked as a carpenter until he was thirty years old. (Amen) Then for three years, he just got on his feet, and he was an itinerant preacher. And he went about doing some things. He didn't have much. He never wrote a book. He never held an office. He never had a family. (Yes) He never owned a house. He never went to college. He never visited a big city. He never went two hundred miles from where he was born. He did none of the usual things that the world would associate with greatness. He had no credentials but himself.

He was only thirty-three when the tide of public opinion turned against him. They called him a rabble-rouser. They called him a troublemaker. They said he was an agitator. (Glory to God) He practiced civil disobedience; he broke injunctions. And so he was turned over to his enemies and went through the mockery of a trial. And the irony of it all is that his friends turned him over to them. (Amen)

One of his closest friends denied him. Another of his friends turned him over to his enemies. And while he was dying, the people who killed him gambled for his clothing, the only possession that he had in the world. (Lord help him) When he was dead he was buried in a borrowed tomb, through the pity of a friend.

Nineteen centuries have come and gone and today he stands as the most influential figure that ever entered human history. All of the armies that ever marched, all the navies that ever sailed, all the parliaments that ever sat, and all the kings that ever reigned put together (Yes) have not affected the life of man on this earth (Amen) as much as that one solitary life. His name may be a familiar one. (Jesus) But today, I can hear them talking about him. Every now and then somebody says, "He's King of Kings." (Yes) And again I can hear somebody saying,

"He's Lord of Lords." Somewhere else I can hear somebody saying, "In Christ there is no East nor West." (Yes) And then they go on and talk about, "In Him there's no North and South, but one great Fellowship of Love throughout the whole wide world." He didn't have anything. (Amen) He just went around serving and doing good.

This morning, you can be on his right hand and his left hand if you serve. (Amen) It's the only way in. Every now and then I guess we all think realistically (Yes, sir) about that day when we will be victimized with what is life's final common denominator—that something that we call death.

We all think about it. And every now and then I think about my own death and I think about my own funeral. And I don't think of it in a morbid sense. And every now and then I ask myself, "What is it that I would want said?" And I leave the word to you this morning.

If any of you are around when I have to meet my day, I don't want a long funeral. And if you get somebody to deliver the eulogy, tell them not to talk too long. (Yes) And every now and then I wonder what I want them to say. Tell them not to mention that I have a Nobel Peace Prize—that isn't important. Tell them not to mention that I have three or four hundred other awards—that's not important. Tell them not to mention where I went to school. (Yes)

I'd like somebody to mention that day that Martin Luther King, Jr., tried to give his life serving others. (Yes)

I'd like for somebody to say that day that Martin Luther King, Jr., tried to love somebody.

I want you to say that day that I tried to be right on the war question. (Amen)

I want you to be able to say that day that I did try to feed the hungry. (Yes)

And I want you to be able to say that day that I did try in my life to clothe those who were naked. (Yes)

I want you to say on that day that I did try in my life to visit those who were in prison. (Lord)

I want you to say that I tried to love and serve humanity. (Yes)

Yes, if you want to say that I was a drum major, say that I was a drum major for justice. (Amen) Say that I was a drum major for peace. (Yes)

I was a drum major for righteousness. And all of the other shallow things will not matter. (Yes) I won't have any money to leave behind. I won't have the fine and luxurious things of life to leave behind.

But I just want to leave a committed life behind. (Amen) And that's all I want to say.

If I can help somebody as I pass along,

If I can cheer somebody with a word or song,

If I can show somebody he's traveling wrong,

Then my living will not be in vain.

If I can do my duty as a Christian ought,

If I can bring salvation to a world once wrought,

If I can spread the message as the master taught,

Then my living will not be in vain.

Yes, Jesus, I want to be on your right or your left side, (Yes) not for any selfish reason.

I want to be on your right or your left side, not in terms of some political kingdom or ambition. But I just want to be there in love and in justice and truth and in commitment to others, so that we can make this old world a new world.

(Delivered at Ebenezer Baptist Church, Atlanta, Georgia, on 4 February 1968.)

There it goes. There is nothing wrong with desiring greatness. It is the noblest desire. It just needs to be re-defined. Just like we have perverted many things in this world, greatness has been done so even worse.

We define it by what a man can take instead of what a man can give. We define it by the dominance of men instead of by their service to mankind.

We consider Genkhis Khan and Napoleon Bonaparte as great, and we overlook Mother Theresa and Martin Luther King Jr.

It gratifies one to know that Christ does not condemn the drum major instinct. It is a very human instinct. He just admonishes us, 'Whosoever would be the greatest amongst us must be the servant of all.'

14 GIVE US THIS DAY

Carpe diem - Seize the day

A bird does not sing because it has an answer. It sings because it has a song. - **Chinese Proverb**

We have made the word emotion carry a negative connotation over time. Yet, there is nothing wrong with emotions. When you say, 'so and so is emotional,' usually, we imagine somebody who is explosive in a negative way.

Emotions are simply feelings. There are, therefore, good emotions and bad emotions. The coinage of the word Emotional Quotient (EQ) came many years after its cousin Intelligence Quotient (IQ). So it took humanity decades to realise that emotions are just about as important as intelligence.

Peter Salovey and John D. Mayer coined the term 'Emotional Intelligence' only in 1990, describing it as "a form of social intelligence that involves the ability to monitor one's own and others' feelings and emotions, to discriminate among them, and to use this information to guide one's thinking and action", while the first modern intelligence test in history (IQ) was developed in 1904, by Alfred Binet (1857-1911) and Theodore Simon (1873-1961).

Your emotional prosperity should supersede everything you do

The beautiful thing about emotions as against intelligence is that they can be managed and controlled. You can actually prepare your emotions for positivity every day through prayer, devotion and meditation. These will help get you in tune with your days. Your inner vision should guide your life to your desired shores, but a bubbling soul is your fuel for each day.

We need to have this deep sense of enjoyment of the work we do towards achieving our lives' goals.

Rewards, money and recognition should be secondary in this equation. We must first and foremost be driven by the love for what we do. Life is a journey where we often reach climaxes, but life is not the climaxes but the journey. If you enjoy the journey even before and after the climaxes, then you are living the life.

Bear the image of a happy child

"He called a little child to him and placed the child among them, and he said: Truly I tell you, unless you change and become like little children, you will never enter the Kingdom of heaven. Therefore, whoever takes the lowly position of this child is the greatest in the Kingdom of heaven."

Children's state of joy is influenced by their trust and knowing that their wishes will deliver in accordance with their expectations. That's joyful living no-frills, just being happy. You want to enter your Kingdom of peace and prosperity; your life must bear that image of a happy child.

So life is nothing but a journey in pursuit of one's inner peace and true wellbeing, and when you find it, you become unstoppable. Trust the Lord's timing, for He says, 'When the time is right, I the Lord will make it happen.' So trust the timing of the Lord. This is the faith that brings the rain.

When you start a new day, have awareness and open your heart to the move of the moment. It may be the time to be propelled.

As you start your day in devotion, you are inviting spiritual powers to bring you in to your place of self-awareness. Being aware of who you are, increases your *present-ness*, which builds your self-confidence. You then glow and immerse yourself into a deeper light that ushers you into the beauty of the day and life. All these manifest in the morning. As the Bible says, "Joy cometh in the morning."

Knowing that *'joy cometh in the morning'* will assist you in pursuing life with greater determination and a drive to succeed, not propelled by some 'must do list' or routine or job requirements but by purpose.

When we start our day like that, it becomes a constant reminder that we are called to a higher life—a life of great possibilities and of better promises. Throughout your day, you need to place your faith in a permanent place of peace and prosperity. Whatever the difficulty, we have no option but to arise and shine. People with happy attitudes like that, who embrace the day like budding would-be flowers in the morning, I have found to be teachable and easy to assist.

A teachable spirit learns that "What I couldn't do well yesterday, today is a new opportunity to make up." Life has a way of granting us fresh starts when God redeems our lost days. If we lose our shine, and we are on the verge of defeat, somewhat life has a way of restoring us into a new day that dawns. Such moments are never to be wasted or left unexploited.

So light up that lamp!

Never outsource your happiness to people or circumstances that are not part of the journey towards your happiness.

A new day is the key to unlock your purpose, where you pray: "Our Father in heaven, hallowed be your name. Your Kingdom come, your will be done, on earth as it is in heaven. Give us this day our daily bread, and forgive us our debts, as we also have forgiven our debtors. And lead us not into temptation, but deliver us from evil.

But more than everything else, pray unto the Father and say, "Give us this day."

This deep sense of reliance on God and our faith helps us each day to believe that we have our daily provisions set aside. It moves us away from the realm of lack into a dimension of abundance. Yet 'even the young lions they suffer hunger, but they that seek the Lord lack no good thing.'

ABOUT

The Author

The little things we do add up to our big ideas, our goals and aspirations. You can do so much more with littleness. - **Vusi Mashabane**

Vusi Mashabane is a Futurist and an Enlightened Entrepreneur, who is passionate about help build organisations that make a difference to humanity. An eternal optimist with natural-born leadership attributes with excellent strategic planning and communications abilities. He has served in various leadership portfolios at his alma mater, in different capacities.

He holds a Masters Degree in Development Economics (MDev), cum laude in Leadership and Financial Management (UL) . He has a Bachelor's Degree in Administration and Project Management Certificate (Wits). He has been involved in Management Consulting for over 20 years.

Vusi is the Executive Chairman of Mohlaloga Group, a Management Consulting firm with various interests in real estate, media and hospitality. He also serves in different Boards of Companies, State-Owned Entities and JSE listed companies in various roles. An avid reader who enjoys leading as the Spiritual Leader of COTH Polokwane.

He is married to Molatelo, an attorney by profession, and together they have two wonderful children Kgoši and Khaya.

BIBLIOGRAPHY

References & Citations

Lerner, Michael. "God and Goddess Emerging." Tikkun, vol. 29, no. 3, Institute of Labor and Mental Health, July 2014, p. 23.

Mahoney, Ashley. "JCSU Needs All Hands on Deck to Make a Difference." The Charlotte Post, vol. 42, no. 25, Charlotte Post Publishing Co., 23 Feb. 2017, p. 5A.

Smith, Tracy. "Living, Loving, and Leading in the Wild and Dazzling Middle Grades: An Open Letter to Prospective and Newer Middle Grades Teachers." Middle School Journal, vol. 48, no. 2, Association for Middle Level Education, Mar. 2017, p. 2.

Ryken, Philip, et al. "Christ-Centered Presidency: The Threefold Office of Christ as a Theological Paradigm for Leading a Christian College/Response/ Response/Response/Response/Author's Response to Comments." Christian Scholar's Review, vol. 47, no. 2, Christian Scholar's Review, Jan. 2018, p. 107.

Johnson, Shontavia. "America's Always Been a Hotbed for Black Inventors." The Triangle Tribune, vol. 20, no. 50, Charlotte Post Publishing Co., 24 Mar. 2019, p. 2A.

I O G R A P H Y. https://orcaslibrary.org/docs/bhm/Famous%20BHM.pdf

Frykholm, Amy. "God Help the Child." The Christian Century, vol. 132, no. 9, Christian Century Foundation, Apr. 2015, p. 39.

"'For I Know the Plans I Have for You,' Declares the LORD, 'Plans to Prosper You and Not to Harm You, Plans to Give You Hope and a Future.'" Florida Times Union, Florida Times Union, 12 June 2021, p. B-6.

Shareef, Nadiyah, and Demetria Farve. "PPP by BIG: 'Preparing for Phenomenal Progress' by 'Bridging the Intergenerational Gap' - Part II." Muslim Journal, vol. 43, no. 32, Muslim Journal, 27 Apr. 2018, p. 9.

Murphey, Dwight. "The Specter of Capital." The Journal of Social, Political, and Economic Studies, vol. 40, no. 1/2, Council for Social and Economic Studies, Inc., Apr. 2015, p. 129.

Treier, Daniel. "The Gift of Finitude: Wisdom from Ecclesiastes for a Theology of Education." Christian Scholar's Review, vol. 48, no. 4, Christian Scholar's Review, July 2019, p. 371.

SETTING NEW PATTERNS IN PSYCHIATRIC RESEARCH. https://media.nature.com/original/magazine-assets/d42473-020-00027-w/d42473-020-00027-w.pdf

Grant, Lynda. "Fear Is Our Faith Working in Reverse." The Charlotte Post, vol. 39, no. 26, Charlotte Post Publishing Co., 6 Mar. 2014, p. 3B.

Freedom from the Press: Journalism and State Power in https://core.ac.uk/download/pdf/233620761.pdf

Tapley, Patti. "Student Engagement Begins With You!" Techniques, vol. 91, no. 2, Association for Career & Technical Education, Feb. 2016, p. 28.

Horton, Michael. "Lord And Giver Of Life": The Holy Spirit In Redemptive History." Journal of the Evangelical Theological Society, vol. 62, no. 1, Evangelical Theological Society, Mar. 2019, p. 47.

The KING'S Medium Term Plan History. https://www.kingswarrington.com/wp-content/uploads/2016/04/History_Yr8_LC2.pdf

Saliers, Don. "Mary Oliver's Magnificat." The American Organist, vol. 53, no. 4, American Guild of Organists, Apr. 2019, p. 10.

Hillary Climbs Mt. Everest. http://hlrgazette.com/2011-articles/144-april-23-2011/1511-hillary-climbs-mt-everest.pdf

Bennett, Leigh, and Steve Hemenway. "Gender Differences in Law Enforcement." Sheriff, vol. 67, no. 2, National Sheriff's Association, Mar. 2015, p. 70.

Arnold, Jeff, and Jeff Arnold. *"A Summons to Subversive Christianity."* The *Hutchinson News, GateHouse Media, Inc., 3 Dec. 2016, p. n/a.*

2 Kings 4:26 Context: Please run now to meet her, and ask her, 'Is it well with you? Is it well with your husband? Is it well with the child?'" She answered, "It is well." (n.d.). https://biblehub.com/context/2_kings/4-26.htm.

2008 global financial crisis: Acumen - Knowledge without boundaries. Acumen. (n.d.). https://acumenias.in/current-affairs-detail/2008-global-financial-crisis.

Annemareerowley, Annemareerowley, & 9, H. on A. (2018, April 8). *An Eloquent Offering...* coolcalmandconnected. https://coolcalmandconnected.com/2018/04/09/an-eloquent-offering/.

Bible Gateway passage: Matthew 18:2-3 - New International Version. Bible Gateway. (n.d.). https://www.biblegateway.com/passage/?search=Matthew+18%3A2-3&version=NIV.

Bingham, J., Martin.parnell, Morrison, T., Vujicic, N., J.R.R.Tolkien, Weller, T., Nathan, N., Ondra, A., Anker, C., Rubin, M., Hincks, A. T., Finlay, B., Pierre Alexandre Jean Mollière - French playwright, Kilian Jornet – Elite Mountain Runner, Rogers, M., King, S., Ban Ki Moon – Secretary General of the United Nations, Beta, T., William Arthur Ward – American Author, & Tracy, B. (n.d.). *Martin Parnell Finish the Race Attitude.* Martin Parnell - Finish the Race Attitude. http://www.martinparnell.com/blog.

Cartwright, M. (2021, July 6). *Mapungubwe.* World History Encyclopedia. https://www.worldhistory.org/Mapungubwe/.

The Drum Major Instinct. The Martin Luther King, Jr., Research and Education Institute. (2014, July 9). https://kinginstitute.stanford.edu/king-papers/publications/knock-midnight-inspiration-great-sermons-reverend-martin-luther-king-jr-8.

Griswold, R. (2016, April 6). *R GRISWOLD.* Ready Made Resources. https://readymaderesources.com/robert-kiyosaki-and-harry-dent-warn-that-financial-armageddon-is-imminent-michael-snyder/.

How to Manage Your Anger Issues. pursueGOD.org. (2019, May 31). https://www.pursuegod.org/how-to-manage-your-anger-issues/.

Hyper Effects. (2021, June 12). *Hyper Effects Explain The Success Story Of Elon Reeve Musk.* Hyper Effects. https://hypereffects.com/business/success-story-of-elon-musk/.

It Is Well With My Soul - Lyrics, Hymn Meaning and Story. GodTube. (n.d.). https://www.godtube.com/popular-hymns/it-is-well-with-my-soul/.

Kirkpatrick, D. (2020, February 1). *Emotional Intelligence*. Life Skills Weekly. https://lifeskillsweekly.com/emotional-intelligence/.

Koll, D., & David Koll is pastor of Anaheim (Calif.) Christian Reformed Church. (n.d.). *The Lord, Our Shepherd: A Series for Lent and Easter Based on Psalm 23*. The Lord, Our Shepherd: A Series for Lent and Easter Based on Psalm 23 | Reformed Worship. https://www.reformedworship.org/article/december-2002/lord-our-shepherd-series-lent-and-easter-based-psalm-23.

Lasco, G. (1970, January 1). *The apocryphal Fernando Pessoa and the imagined Pope Francis*. Gideon Lasco's Medical Anthropology Page. https://www.gideonlasco.com/2015/12/the-apocryphal-fernando-pessoa-and.html.

Matthew 6:13 And lead us not into temptation, but deliver us from the evil one.'. (n.d.). https://www.biblehub.com/matthew/6-13.htm.

Matthew 6:26 Look at the birds of the air: They do not sow or reap or gather into barns--and yet your heavenly Father feeds them. Are you not much more valuable than they? (n.d.). https://www.biblehub.com/matthew/6-26.htm.

MATTHEW 6:34 KJV Take therefore no thought for the morrow: for the morrow shall take thought for the things of itself.... MATTHEW 6:34 KJV "Take therefore no thought for the morrow: for the morrow shall take thought for the things of itself...." (n.d.). https://www.kingjamesbibleonline.org/Matthew-6-34/.

New York : Viking. (1970, January 1). *Too big to fail : the inside story of how Wall Street and Washington fought to save the financial system--and themselves : Sorkin, Andrew Ross : Free Download, Borrow, and Streaming*. Internet Archive. https://archive.org/details/toobigtofailinsi00sork.

Perspective. Hopkins Fundraising. (n.d.). https://www.hopkinsfundraising.com/perspective/.

Psalm 23:4 Even though I walk through the valley of the shadow of death, I will fear no evil, for You are with me; Your rod and Your staff, they comfort me. (n.d.). https://www.biblehub.com/psalms/23-4.htm.

quoteresearch, A. (2019, July 29). *A Bird Doesn't Sing Because It Has an Answer, It Sings Because It Has a Song*. Quote Investigator. https://quoteinvestigator.com/2015/12/03/bird-sing/.

Revelation 1:18 - Verse-by-Verse Bible Commentary. StudyLight.org. (n.d.). https://www.studylight.org/commentary/revelation/1-18.html.

Rockets To Riches: The Rise And Rise Of Elon Musk. Forbes Africa. (2021, February 4). https://www.forbesafrica.com/cover-story/2021/02/05/rockets-to-riches-the-rise-and-rise-of-elon-musk/.

Scribd. (n.d.). *Holiday 2011 Emma*. Scribd. https://de.scribd.com/doc/151060952/Holiday-2011-Emma.

See Mount Everest from a Motorcycle! HAULBIKES. (2020, January 17). https://haulbikes.com/see-mount-everest-from-a-motorcycle/.

There are some men who lift the age they inhabit, till all men walk on higher ground in that lifetime. SmartBrief. (2018, January 9). https://www.smartbrief.com/branded/14B53D24-35C5-41D4-B190-AC51C762248C/F1F5E6D5-F9C0-4EC1-8830-6F3B5F8C73EA.

User. (2016, May 19). *The Fear of Failure*. ViddyAd. https://viddyad.com/the-fear-of-failure/.

Wikimedia Foundation. (2006, February 16). *Edmond hillary*. Wikipedia. https://en.wikipedia.org/wiki/Edmond_hillary.

Wikimedia Foundation. (2021, July 6). *Bankruptcy of Lehman Brothers*. Wikipedia. https://en.wikipedia.org/wiki/Bankruptcy_of_Lehman_Brothers.

Wikimedia Foundation. (2021, March 14). *Nazarene movement*. Wikipedia. https://en.wikipedia.org/wiki/Nazarene_movement.

/* inline tdc_css att */.tdi_81_00e{margin-bottom:2px !important;}/* portrait */@media (min-width: 768px) and (max-width: 1018px) {.tdi_81_00e{margin-bottom:0px !important;}}/* custom css */.tdi_81_00e{ display: inline-block; , Tyson, J., By, Tyson, J., Alecia M. White - Jun 29, -, A. M. W., 24, K. B.- J., -, K. B., 21, E. S.- J., -, E. S., /* inline tdc_css att */.tdi_105_004{margin-bottom:0px !important;}/* custom css */.tdi_105_004{ padding: 21px; border: 0px solid #ededed; }.tdi_105_004 .tdb-author-photo{ , Jeannette TysonI'm Jeannette! Saved by grace at 19 and doing my best to live for the Lord after years of trying things my way. One beautiful daughter, I'm Jeannette! Saved by grace at 19 and doing my best to live for the Lord after years of trying things my way. One beautiful daughter, 23, K. B.- J., -, K. B., Kim Brightness - Jun 4, Team Jesus - Apr 14, -, T. J., Team Jesus - Mar 24, ... Alecia M. White - Jun 18. (2018, February 12). *5 Red Flags to Distinguish Walking by Faith vs. Fear*. Team Jesus Magazine. https://teamjesusmag.com/5-red-flags-to-distinguish-walking-by-faith-vs-fear/.

1 John 2:14 I have written to you, fathers, because you know Him who is from the beginning. I have written to you, young men, because you are strong, and the word of God abides in you, and you have overcome the evil one. (n.d.). https://www.biblehub.com/1_john/2-14.htm.

7. *The Fulfillment of the Davidic Covenant*. 7. The Fulfillment of the Davidic Covenant | Bible.org. (n.d.). https://bible.org/seriespage/7-fulfillment-davidic-covenant.

A&E Networks Television. (2021, February 2). *Madam C.J. Walker*. Biography. com. https://www.biography.com/people/madam-cj-walker-9522174.

Atlantis facts for kids. Atlantis Facts for Kids. (n.d.). https://kids.kiddle.co/Atlantis.

Carlyle, T. (2019, August 8). *Reduce Worry by Living in 'Day-tight Compartments'*. Dale Carnegie Training of Central & Southern New Jersey. http://www.dalecarnegiewaynj.com/2011/05/27/reduce-worry-by-living-in-day-tight-compartments/.

Chapter 1, Verses 1 to 31. Condensed Bible - Genesis. (n.d.). http://www.condensedbible.com/page4.html.

Collins, P., says, B. M., Michelle, B., says, P. C., Sandra at Thistle Cove Farm says, Farm, S. at T. C., says, P., & Pcollins. (n.d.). *Brandi Michelle*. Gift of Simple. https://www.giftofsimple.com/mustard-seed-faith/.

Dooley, M., & Proctor, B. (2019). *Infinite possibilities: the art of living your dreams*. Amazon. https://www.amazon.com/Infinite-Possibilities-Living-Your-Dreams/dp/1582702322.

Drye, W. (2021, May 4). *Explaining the Legend of Atlantis*. History. https://www.nationalgeographic.com/history/article/atlantis.

Foundation, W. (Ed.). (2021, July 6). *Pre-Raphaelite Brotherhood*. Wikipedia. https://en.wikipedia.org/wiki/Pre-Raphaelite_Brotherhood.

Goodreads. (1970, January 1). *The African Americans: Many Rivers to Cross by Henry Louis Gates Jr*. Goodreads. https://www.goodreads.com/book/show/18559600-the-african-americans.

Goodreads. (n.d.). *A quote by Ellen DeGeneres*. Goodreads. https://www.goodreads.com/quotes/86174-in-the-beginning-there-was-nothing-god-said-let-there.

Goodreads. (n.d.). *A quote by Henry David Thoreau*. Goodreads. https://www.goodreads.com/quotes/51150-i-once-had-a-sparrow-alight-upon-my-shoulder-for.

Goodreads. (n.d.). *A quote by Peter M. Senge*. Goodreads. https://www.goodreads.com/quotes/19854-people-with-high-levels-of-personal-mastery-cannot-afford-to-choose.

Goodreads. (n.d.). *A quote by Ralph Waldo Emerson*. Goodreads. https://www.goodreads.com/quotes/876-to-be-yourself-in-a-world-that-is-constantly-trying.

Goodreads. (n.d.). *A quote by Winston S. Churchill*. Goodreads. https://www.goodreads.com/quotes/21921-the-empires-of-the-future-are-the-empires-of-the.

Google. (n.d.). *The Inventive Spirit of African Americans*. Google Books. https://books.google.com/books?id=Wz-DTSXeLRYC&pg=PA31&lpg=PA31&dq=Oscar%2BStewart%2BNed%2Bpatent&source=bl&ots=4AuokDOGVw&sig=p_jIR4bYZPFDk0tnNh74gSae-mI&hl=en&sa=X&ved=0ahUKEwi3i-vq5oHSAhUD5YMKHXoeDVQ4ChDoAQgxMAg#v=onepage?xid=PS_smithsonian.

The Instructive, Commanding, Comforting and Encouraging Word of God!!! Christ's Kingdom and the End Times. (2020, August 5). https://christskingdom.org/articles/instructive-commanding-comforting-encouraging-word-god/.

Isbouts, J.-P. (2021, May 3). *How King David ascended to the throne of Israel*. Culture. https://www.nationalgeographic.com/culture/article/story-king-david-goliath.

It's not that some people have willpower and some don't. It's that some people are ready to change and others are not. James Gordon: It's not that some people have willpower and some don't. It's that some people are ready to change and others are not. (n.d.). https://www.quotes.net/quote/20444.

Johanna. (2016, July 29). *Change is the constant, the signal for rebirth, the egg of the phoenix. - Christina Baldwin*. One Idea Away. https://www.oneideaaway.com/quote/change-constant-signal-rebirth-egg-phoenix-christina-baldwin/.

Jonson, B. (n.d.). *To the Memory of My Beloved the Author, Mr....* Poetry Foundation. https://www.poetryfoundation.org/poems/44466/to-the-memory-of-my-beloved-the-author-mr-william-shakespeare.

Klerk, M. de. (1970, January 1). *To Muse and Abuse*. 2015. https://to-muse-and-abuse.blogspot.com/2015/.

Little by little by Shinku. a poem by Shinku - All Poetry. (n.d.). https://

allpoetry.com/poem/11353882-Little-by-little-by-Shinku.

Luke 1:33 and He will reign over the house of Jacob forever. His kingdom will never end!". (n.d.). https://biblehub.com/luke/1-33.htm.

Lynn, S. (2019, April 8). *Black History Month: Inventions Made by Black Slaves Denied Patents*. Black Enterprise. https://www.blackenterprise.com/black-history-month-inventions-black-slaves-denied-patents/.

MARK 11:23 KJV For verily I say unto you, That whosoever shall say unto this mountain, Be thou removed, and be thou... MARK 11:23 KJV "For verily I say unto you, That whosoever shall say unto this mountain, Be thou removed, and be thou...". (n.d.). https://www.kingjamesbibleonline.org/Mark-11-23/.

Mark 1:44 "Don't tell this to anyone," he said. "Go and show yourself to the priest. Offer the sacrifices that Moses commanded. It will be a witness to the priest and the people that you are 'clean.' ": New International Reader's Version (NIRV): Download The Bible App Now. Mark 1:44 "Don't tell this to anyone," he said. "Go and show yourself to the priest. Offer the sacrifices that Moses commanded. It will be a witness to the priest and the people that you are 'clean.' " | New International Reader's Version (NIRV) | Download The Bible App Now. (n.d.). https://www.bible.com/bible/110/MRK.1.44.NIRV.

Opondo, P. (2021, April 27). *Only the paranoid survive, so let Ndegwa be*. The Standard. https://www.standardmedia.co.ke/editorial/article/2001411117/only-the-paranoid-survive-so-let-ndegwa-be.

Perdue, S. M. (2014, September 19). English Blog. https://sites.psu.edu/rclperdue/2014/09/19/the-big-three-of-greek-philosophy-socrates-plato-and-aristotle/.

Proverbs 4:23 Guard your heart with all diligence, for from it flow springs of life. (n.d.). https://biblehub.com/proverbs/4-23.htm.

Psalm 89 Commentary. Sermon Writer. (2019, September 1). https://sermonwriter.com/biblical-commentary/old-testament-psalm-89-commentary/.

Psalm 8:5 You made him a little lower than the angels; You crowned him with glory and honor. (n.d.). https://www.biblehub.com/psalms/8-5.htm.

Quotations by Ellen DeGeneres. Ellen DeGeneres Quotes - The Quotations Page. (n.d.). http://www.quotationspage.com/quotes/Ellen_DeGeneres/.

r/nocontext - In the beginning, it was not quite very sweet. Then god said, "let there be the sweetness akin to balls". And so it was. The world, now bathed in ball-like sweetness, was empty, and so god created the heavens and the earth, different only in how sweet one can compare each in relation to balls. reddit. (n.d.). https://www.reddit.com/r/nocontext/ comments/20qtgb/in_the_beginning_it_was_not_quite_very_sweet_ then/.

Sev, T. (2017, February 28). *The System and the End Times*. The Sevan Seas. https://thesevanseas.wordpress.com/2017/02/27/the-system-and-the-end-times/.

Shelley, P. B. (n.d.). *Adonais: An Elegy on the Death of John Keats by...* Poetry Foundation. https://www.poetryfoundation.org/poems/45112/ adonais-an-elegy-on-the-death-of-john-keats.

Shuck, J. (1970, January 1). And David Danced--A Sermon. https:// zacharyshuck.blogspot.com/2012/08/and-david-danced-sermon.html.

Simon, S. (2019, November 30). *Deep Political Rifts Often Have Led U.S. To Transformation, Researcher Says*. NPR. https://www.npr. org/2019/11/30/783819956/deep-political-rifts-often-have-led-u-s-to-transformation-researcher-say.

Take Back Your Power. Proctor Gallagher Institute. (2016, April 15). https:// www.proctorgallagherinstitute.com/10843/take-back-your-power.

Tracy. (2019, February 16). *5 Inventions By Enslaved Black Men Blocked By U.S. Patent Office*. Atlanta Black Star. http://atlantablackstar. com/2014/02/11/5-inventions-by-enslaved-black-men-blocked-by-us-patent-office/4/?xid=PS_smithsonian.

What does it mean to love your neighbour as you love yourself? Mohammed Amin's website - Serious writing for serious readers. (2018, May 30). https://www.mohammedamin.com/Community_issues/Love-your-neighbour.html.

What If Your Life Was Full of Endless Possibilities ... (n.d.). https://www. psychologytoday.com/us/blog/high-octane-women/201201/what-if-your-life-was-full-endless-possibilities.

Wikimedia Foundation. (2021, February 14). *Frederic George Stephens*. Wikipedia. https://en.wikipedia.org/wiki/Frederic_George_Stephens.

Wikimedia Foundation. (2021, July 5). *John Everett Millais*. Wikipedia. https://en.wikipedia.org/wiki/John_Everett_Millais.

Wikimedia Foundation. (2021, July 6). *Pre-Raphaelite Brotherhood*. Wikipedia.

https://en.wikipedia.org/wiki/Pre-Raphaelite_Brotherhood.

Wikimedia Foundation. (2021, June 11). *Enron scandal*. Wikipedia. https://en.wikipedia.org/wiki/Enron_scandal.

Wikimedia Foundation. (2021, June 23). *Thomas Woolner*. Wikipedia. https://en.wikipedia.org/wiki/Thomas_Woolner.

Wikimedia Foundation. (2021, June 28). *Dante Gabriel Rossetti*. Wikipedia. https://en.wikipedia.org/wiki/Dante_Gabriel_Rossetti.

Wikimedia Foundation. (2021, June 30). *James Collinson*. Wikipedia. https://en.wikipedia.org/wiki/James_Collinson.

Wikimedia Foundation. (2021, June 7). *William Michael Rossetti*. Wikipedia. https://en.wikipedia.org/wiki/William_Michael_Rossetti.

Witter, B. (2021, January 28). *10 Black Inventors Who Changed Your Life*. Biography.com. https://www.biography.com/news/madam-cj-walker-black-inventors.

Xplore. (n.d.). *Lao Tzu Quotes*. BrainyQuote. https://www.brainyquote.com/quotes/lao_tzu_137141.

LITTL꒒ by LITTL꒒

JOIN THE CONVERSATION

Visit www.littlebylittle.co.za for more information.

redOystor

AN INVITATION FROM THE PUBLISHER

Join us at www.redoystor.com or connect with us on facebook, instagram and twitter @redOystor to be part of a community of people who love the very best in books and reading.

Whether you want to discover more about the author or the book, read more about upcoming events, interviews or watch trailers, or have a chance to win early limited editions, we think you will like what you are looking for.

And if you don't, let us know what's missing through our contact us page or email us at **theEditor@redoystor.com**

We love what we do, and we'd love you to be a part of it.

www.redoystor.com

www.ingramcontent.com/pod-product-compliance
Lightning Source LLC
Chambersburg PA
CBHW020153090426
42734CB00008B/805